Betty Crocker
a piece of cake

Easy Cakes—from Dump Cakes
to Mug Cakes, Slow-Cooker
Cakes and More!

Houghton Mifflin Harcourt
Boston • New York • 2018

GENERAL MILLS

Global Business Solutions Director:
Heather Polen

Global Business Solutions Manager:
Maja Qamar

Executive Editor: Cathy Swanson

Recipe Development and Testing: Betty
Crocker Kitchens

Photography: General Mills Photography
Studios and Image Library

HOUGHTON MIFFLIN HARCOURT

Editor-in-Chief: Deb Brody

Executive Editor: Anne Ficklen

Editorial Assistant: Claire Safran

Managing Editor: Marina Padakis

Production Editor: Helen Seachrist

Cover Design: Tai Blanche

Interior Design and Layout: Tai Blanche

Senior Production Coordinator:
Kimberly Kiefer

For information about permission to reproduce selections from this book, write to Permissions, Houghton Mifflin Harcourt Publishing Company, 3 Park Avenue, New York, New York 10016.

hmhco.com

Library of Congress Cataloging-in-Publication Data is available.

ISBN 978-1-328-91848-2 (paperback); 978-1-328-91844-4 (ebook)

Manufactured in China

SCP 10 9 8 7 6 5 4 3 2 1

Cover photo: (clockwise from top left) Slow-Cooker Zebra Cake (page 190); Unicorn Doughnut Cake (page 276); Spiced Pumpkin–Chocolate Chip Mug Cake (page 118); Candy Bar Ice-Cream Cake 'Wiches (page 162)

Interior background photo: © Ursa Major/ Shutterstock.com

The Betty Crocker Kitchens seal guarantees success in your kitchen. Every recipe has been tested in America's Most Trusted Kitchens™ to meet our high standards of reliability, easy preparation and great taste.

FIND MORE GREAT IDEAS AT
BettyCrocker.com

Dear Sweet Tooths,

Let's be honest. We all have a sweet tooth once in a while! Baking your own cake to satisfy that craving can be easy, gratifying and fun. We take the difficulty out of cake making with this new collection of easy recipes that are . . . well . . . "A Piece of Cake" to make!

From microwavable mug cakes for one or two to slow-cooker cakes, icebox cakes and poke cakes, we've got incredibly delicious and easy ways to satisfy. No traditional two-layer cakes, fancy frostings or difficult decorations here. These cakes are simple to make and wow-worthy enough to tote to all your get-togethers.

Surprise your family with Apple-Spice Bundt Cake with Butterscotch Glaze (page 18). Whip up Strawberry-Pineapple Icebox Cake (page 84) when you want to keep your kitchen cool. Exhilarate your pumpkin-crazy taste buds with Pumpkin-Spiced Creamy Rum Poke Cake (page 104), or Slow-Cooker Peanut Butter Cup Swirl Cake (page 140) can cook away while you play.

Our Fabulous Cake Hacks (page 54) give you all the foolproof secrets you need to bake successful cakes every time. How to Build an Ice-Cream Cake (page 160) shows you how to customize ice-cream cakes for any occasion. And don't miss the Genius Ways to Frost a Cake (page 198), which show you super-easy ways to frost a cake without any special training required.

Let's bake and eat cake!

Betty Crocker

Look for recipes with these icons:

ONE BOWL • **MAKE AHEAD** • **FAST**

CONTENTS

....

Features

Cakes Made Easy

Cake baking doesn't have to challenging or complicated. It's possible to indulge your sweet tooth any time when you know the insider tips and have no-fuss recipes. Whether you make one yourself or invite a friend or child to have fun in the kitchen with you, you'll love the sweet results!

Measure Correctly

When it comes to baking, accuracy is important. Spoon dry ingredients into a dry measuring cup, and level off with a flat-edged utensil. Fill liquid measuring cups with liquid, and check by looking at eye level while the cup sits steady on the counter.

Butter Love

For the best results and flavor, use real butter in recipes calling for butter. Do not use reduced-fat butter or whipped products.

Pan-tastic Results

Use shiny pans that reflect the heat to bake cakes that are tender and light. Dark pans or pans with nonstick coating absorb the heat faster, causing cakes to brown too quickly and creating hard edges.

Doneness + Time

Don't go just by time when baking cakes. If they are underdone, they will sink when cooling. Bake cakes for the minimum time listed in the recipe, then check for doneness using the doneness indicator in the recipe (usually the toothpick test or touching lightly with finger). Bake longer if needed.

Perfect Peaks

Whether using egg whites or whipped cream, knowing how to properly beat ingredients will ensure that your cakes turn out perfectly.

Soft Peaks: Beat just until peaks form but curl over.

Stiff Peaks: Continue beating until peaks stand upright when beaters are removed.

SWEETENED WHIPPED CREAM

For each cup of whipped cream: In chilled, deep bowl, beat ½ cup whipping cream, 1 tablespoon powdered or granulated sugar and ½ teaspoon vanilla with electric mixer on low speed until mixture begins to thicken. Gradually increase speed to high, and beat just until soft peaks form. Do not overbeat, or mixture will curdle.

Easy Scratch Cake Mix

This super-simple mix or its brown sugar variation is the start of several recipes in this book. Make up a batch to keep on hand to make homemade cakes anytime you're craving something sweet.

PREP TIME: 5 Minutes
START TO FINISH: 5 Minutes

FOR MAKING 2 CUPS CAKE MIX

1⅓	cups all-purpose flour
¾	cup sugar
1¼	teaspoons baking powder
¼	teaspoon salt

FOR MAKING 8 CUPS CAKE MIX

5⅓	cups all-purpose flour
3	cups sugar
5	teaspoons baking powder
1	teaspoon salt

1 In medium or large bowl, mix ingredients for either 2 cups cake mix or 8 cups cake mix until well blended. Use immediately for any recipe in this book calling for Easy Scratch Cake Mix. Or store in tightly covered container in cool, dark location up to 1 month, or freeze up to 3 months.

Easy Brown Sugar Scratch Cake Mix:
Substitute brown sugar for the sugar.

cakes with fruit

Apple Crisp Cake

24 servings | PREP TIME: 30 Minutes | START TO FINISH: 2 Hours 20 Minutes

STREUSEL

- ¾ cup old-fashioned oats
- ¼ cup all-purpose flour
- ¾ cup packed brown sugar
- 1 teaspoon ground cinnamon
- ½ cup cold butter
- ½ cup chopped walnuts

APPLE LAYER

- 1 tablespoon butter
- 2 cups coarsely chopped, peeled tart apples (2 medium)

CAKE

- 1 box yellow cake mix with pudding
- ⅓ cup vegetable oil
- ½ cup water
- 4 eggs
- 1 cup sour cream
- 1 tablespoon ground cinnamon

CINNAMON WHIPPED CREAM

- 1 cup heavy whipping cream
- 2 tablespoons powdered sugar
- ½ teaspoon ground cinnamon
- ½ teaspoon vanilla

1 Heat oven to 350°F. Grease bottom and sides of 13 × 9-inch pan with shortening or spray with cooking spray.

2 In medium bowl, mix oats, flour, brown sugar and 1 teaspoon cinnamon. Cut in ½ cup cold butter, using fork or pastry blender, until mixture is crumbly. Stir in nuts; set aside.

3 In 10-inch nonstick skillet, cook 1 tablespoon butter and the apples over medium heat, stirring frequently, about 5 minutes or until apples are tender. Set aside.

4 In large bowl, beat cake ingredients with electric mixer on medium speed 2 minutes, scraping bowl occasionally. Pour into pan; top evenly with cooked apples. Sprinkle streusel evenly over apples.

5 Bake 44 to 48 minutes or until toothpick inserted in center comes out clean. Remove from oven to cooling rack. Cool completely, about 1 hour. Cut into 6 rows by 4 rows.

6 When ready to serve, in chilled medium bowl, beat whipping cream, powdered sugar, ½ teaspoon cinnamon and the vanilla with electric mixer on low speed until thickened. Gradually increase speed just until stiff peaks form. Top cake with whipped cream.

1 Serving: Calories 260; Total Fat 16g (Saturated Fat 7g, Trans Fat 0g); Cholesterol 60mg; Sodium 180mg; Total Carbohydrate 28g (Dietary Fiber 1g); Protein 2g **Exchanges:** 1 Starch, 1 Other Carbohydrate, 3 Fat **Carbohydrate Choices:** 2

Sweet Secret The tart flavor of Granny Smith apples contrasts with the sweet, spiced cake, but feel free to use your favorite baking apple, such as McIntosh, Braeburn or Jonathan, instead.

Simple Sparkle Top cake pieces with vanilla ice cream in place of whipped cream!

Easy Apple-Walnut Cake

8 servings | PREP TIME: 25 Minutes | START TO FINISH: 1 Hour 30 Minutes

½ cup butter, softened

1 cup sugar

2 eggs

¼ teaspoon vanilla

1¼ cups all-purpose flour

1 teaspoon baking soda

1 teaspoon ground cinnamon

¼ teaspoon salt

1½ cups shredded peeled apples (about 2 medium)

½ cup chopped walnuts

1 quart vanilla or cinnamon ice cream

1 Heat oven to 350°F. Grease 9-inch round pan with shortening; lightly flour.

2 In large bowl, beat butter and sugar with electric mixer on medium speed about 5 minutes or until light and fluffy. Beat in eggs, one at a time. Stir in vanilla, flour, baking soda, cinnamon and salt. Stir in apples and walnuts. Spread into pan.

3 Bake 40 to 45 minutes or until toothpick inserted in center comes out clean. Cool 10 minutes. Remove from pan to cooling rack. Cool 10 minutes longer. Serve warm with ice cream.

1 Serving: Calories 490; Total Fat 25g (Saturated Fat 13g, Trans Fat 0.5g); Cholesterol 115mg; Sodium 380mg; Total Carbohydrate 60g (Dietary Fiber 2g); Protein 7g **Exchanges:** 1½ Starch, 2½ Other Carbohydrate, 5 Fat **Carbohydrate Choices:** 4

Simple Sparkle Add a drizzle of caramel or butterscotch topping on top of the ice cream for an added layer of yum!

Caramel Apple Upside-Down Cake

8 servings | **PREP TIME: 20 Minutes** | **START TO FINISH: 1 Hour 5 Minutes**

TOPPING

3	tablespoons butter
½	cup packed brown sugar
2	tablespoons water
2	medium apples, peeled, cut into ½-inch slices

CAKE

1	cup all-purpose flour
½	teaspoon baking powder
½	teaspoon baking soda
1	teaspoon ground cinnamon
¼	teaspoon ground ginger
¼	teaspoon ground nutmeg
¼	teaspoon salt
⅓	cup butter, softened
½	cup packed brown sugar
2	eggs
½	cup milk

1 Heat oven to 350°F. Grease bottom and side of 9-inch round pan with shortening or spray with cooking spray; line bottom with cooking parchment paper.

2 Place 3 tablespoons butter in pan. Heat in oven until melted. Stir in ½ cup brown sugar and the water. Arrange apple slices over brown sugar mixture; set aside.

3 In small bowl, mix flour, baking powder, baking soda, cinnamon, ginger, nutmeg and salt; set aside. In large bowl, beat ⅓ cup softened butter and ½ cup brown sugar with electric mixer on medium speed, scraping bowl occasionally, about 1 minute or until fluffy. Beat in eggs, one at a time, until smooth. Reduce speed to low. Gradually beat flour mixture into sugar mixture alternately with milk on low speed, beating after each addition, just until smooth. Scrape side of bowl occasionally. Spread batter over apple slices in pan. Tap pan on counter two or three times to eliminate air bubbles from batter.

4 Bake 32 to 38 minutes or until toothpick inserted in center comes out clean. Run knife around side of pan to loosen cake. Cool cake in pan on cooling rack 5 minutes. Place heatproof serving platter upside down over pan; carefully turn platter and pan over. Leave over cake about 1 minute so caramel can drizzle over cake. Remove pan. Serve warm.

1 Serving: Calories 277; Total Fat 14g (Saturated Fat 8g, Trans Fat 0g); Cholesterol 80mg; Sodium 206mg; Total Carbohydrate 36g (Dietary Fiber 1g); Protein 4g **Exchanges:** 1½ Starch, 1½ Other Carbohydrate, 2½ Fat **Carbohydrate Choices:** 3

Simple Sparkle
Serve with Sweetened Whipped Cream (page 6) or vanilla ice cream and additional apple slices to put this dessert over the top.

Slow-Cooker Apple Cake

8 servings | **PREP TIME: 20 Minutes** | **START TO FINISH: 2 Hours**

1½ cups all-purpose flour

⅓ cup packed dark brown sugar

1½ teaspoons ground cinnamon

1 teaspoon baking soda

½ teaspoon baking powder

¼ teaspoon salt

¼ teaspoon ground nutmeg

⅛ teaspoon ground cloves

1 cup unsweetened applesauce

⅓ cup buttermilk

¼ cup butter, melted

1 tablespoon vanilla

1 egg

1 cup dried apple slices, coarsely chopped

1 Spray 5-quart slow cooker with cooking spray. Place 2 (30-inch-long) strips of cooking parchment paper in X pattern in bottom and up side of slow cooker. Line bottom of slow cooker with cooking parchment paper. Spray paper with cooking spray.

2 In medium bowl, stir together flour, brown sugar, cinnamon, baking soda, baking powder, salt, nutmeg and cloves with whisk. In small bowl, mix applesauce, buttermilk, melted butter, vanilla and egg. Add applesauce mixture to flour mixture, stirring until smooth. Stir in dried apples. Pour batter into slow cooker and spread in even layer.

3 Cover; cook on High heat setting 1 hour to 1 hour 30 minutes, carefully rotating slow cooker's ceramic insert 180 degrees (leaving cover on) after every 45 minutes or until puffed and toothpick inserted in center comes out clean. Uncover and transfer ceramic insert from slow cooker to cooling rack. Let stand 10 minutes.

4 Using parchment paper, carefully lift cake out of ceramic insert and transfer to cooling rack. Remove parchment paper. Serve warm.

1 Serving: Calories 240; Total Fat 7g (Saturated Fat 4g, Trans Fat 0g); Cholesterol 40mg; Sodium 340mg; Total Carbohydrate 39g (Dietary Fiber 2g); Protein 4g **Exchanges:** 1 Starch, ½ Fruit, 1 Other Carbohydrate, 1½ Fat **Carbohydrate Choices:** 2½

Sweet Secret If you don't have buttermilk on hand, replace it with 1 teaspoon lemon juice or white vinegar and enough milk to make ⅓ cup.

Simple Sparkle Top servings of cake with dollops of Sweetened Whipped Cream (page 6) and a sprinkle of ground cinnamon or nutmeg.

Apple-Spice Bundt Cake with Butterscotch Glaze

12 servings | PREP TIME: 20 Minutes | START TO FINISH: 2 Hours 20 Minutes

CAKE

- 1 box spice cake mix with pudding
- 1 cup milk
- 3 oz cream cheese (from 8-oz package), softened
- 3 eggs
- 1 large Granny Smith apple, peeled, cored and chopped (2 cups)

BUTTERSCOTCH GLAZE

- 2 tablespoons butter, softened
- 1 cup powdered sugar
- 3 tablespoons butterscotch topping
- 2 tablespoons milk

GARNISH

Dried apple slices, if desired

1 Heat oven to 325°F. Generously grease 10- or 12-cup fluted tube cake pan with shortening.

2 In large bowl, beat all cake ingredients except apple with electric mixer on low speed 1 minute, scraping bowl constantly. Beat on medium speed 2 minutes, scraping bowl occasionally. Stir in apple. Pour into pan.

3 Bake 40 to 45 minutes or until toothpick inserted in center comes out clean. Cool 15 minutes. Place heatproof plate upside down over pan; turn plate and pan over; remove pan. Cool completely, about 1 hour. Place cake on serving plate.

4 In medium bowl, beat butterscotch glaze ingredients with electric mixer on medium speed about 1 minute or until smooth and well combined. Drizzle over top of cake. Garnish with dried apple slices.

1 Serving: Calories 150; Total Fat 6g (Saturated Fat 3.5g, Trans Fat 0g); Cholesterol 60mg; Sodium 110mg; Total Carbohydrate 21g (Dietary Fiber 0g); Protein 3g **Exchanges:** 1 Starch, ½ Other Carbohydrate, 1 Fat **Carbohydrate Choices:** 1½

Sweet Secret Instead of using spice cake mix, use a box of yellow cake mix with pudding and 1½ teaspoons apple pie spice.

Apple-Walnut Cake with Caramel Glaze

16 servings | **PREP TIME: 25 Minutes** | **START TO FINISH: 2 Hours 15 Minutes**

CAKE

- 2 cups packed brown sugar
- 1½ cups vegetable oil
- 3 eggs
- 3 cups all-purpose flour
- 2 teaspoons baking soda
- 2 teaspoons ground cinnamon
- 1 teaspoon ground ginger
- ¼ teaspoon salt
- ¼ teaspoon ground cloves
- 1 cup chopped walnuts
- 2 large apples, peeled, shredded (about 2 cups)

GLAZE

- 2 tablespoons butter, softened
- 1 cup powdered sugar
- 3 tablespoons butterscotch-caramel topping
- 1 tablespoon milk
- Additional ground cinnamon, if desired

1 Heat oven to 350°F. Grease 12-cup fluted tube cake pan with shortening; lightly flour.

2 In large bowl, beat brown sugar, oil and eggs with electric mixer on medium speed until light and fluffy. Add all remaining cake ingredients except walnuts and apples; beat on low speed until smooth. With spoon, gently stir in walnuts and apples. Spoon batter into pan.

3 Bake 1 hour to 1 hour 10 minutes or until toothpick inserted near center comes out clean. Cool 10 minutes. Place heatproof plate upside down over pan; turn plate and pan over. Remove pan. Cool 30 minutes.

4 Meanwhile, in medium bowl, beat all glaze ingredients except cinnamon until smooth. Pour glaze over top of cake, allowing some to run down side. Sprinkle with cinnamon.

1 Serving: Calories 500; Total Fat 28g (Saturated Fat 4.5g, Trans Fat 0g); Cholesterol 45mg; Sodium 240mg; Total Carbohydrate 58g (Dietary Fiber 2g); Protein 5g **Exchanges:** 1 Starch, 3 Other Carbohydrate, 5½ Fat **Carbohydrate Choices:** 4

Sweet Secret If you see spots in the pan where the flour didn't stick, it's because there wasn't any shortening there for it to stick to. Be sure to go over those areas with both shortening and flour before putting the cake batter in the pan so the cake will release cleanly.

Applesauce-Cranberry Cake

16 servings | **PREP TIME: 20 Minutes** | **START TO FINISH: 3 Hours 30 Minutes**

1 tablespoon all-purpose flour

1 cup dried cranberries

2½ cups all-purpose flour

1 tablespoon pumpkin pie spice

1½ teaspoons salt

1 teaspoon baking powder

½ teaspoon baking soda

½ cup butter, softened

1½ cups granulated sugar

2 eggs

1½ cups applesauce

½ cup chopped walnuts or pecans

2 tablespoons powdered sugar

1 Heat oven to 350°F. Grease 12-cup fluted tube cake pan with shortening; lightly flour.

2 In small bowl, toss 1 tablespoon flour and the cranberries to coat; set aside. In large bowl, mix 2½ cups flour, the pumpkin pie spice, salt, baking powder and baking soda; set aside.

3 In another large bowl, beat butter and granulated sugar with electric mixer on low speed 30 seconds, scraping bowl constantly. Beat on high speed until light and fluffy. Beat in eggs, one at a time, until smooth and well blended. On medium speed, gradually beat in flour mixture alternately with applesauce until smooth. Stir in cranberry-flour mixture and nuts. Pour batter into pan.

4 Bake 50 to 60 minutes or until toothpick inserted in center comes out clean. Cool 10 minutes. Remove from pan to cooling rack. Cool completely, about 2 hours. Sprinkle powdered sugar over cake.

1 Serving: Calories 260; Total Fat 9g (Saturated Fat 4g, Trans Fat 0g); Cholesterol 0mg; Sodium 360mg; Total Carbohydrate 44g (Dietary Fiber 1g); Protein 3g **Exchanges:** 1 Starch, ½ Fruit, 1½ Other Carbohydrate, 1½ Fat **Carbohydrate Choices:** 3

Sweet Secret Don't have pumpkin pie spice? Use 1½ teaspoons ground cinnamon, 1 teaspoon ground nutmeg and ¼ teaspoon ground allspice instead.

Warm Caramel Apple Cake

15 servings | **PREP TIME: 20 Minutes** | **START TO FINISH: 1 Hour 20 Minutes**

CAKE

- ½ cup butter
- ¼ cup whipping cream
- 1 cup packed brown sugar
- ½ cup chopped pecans
- 2 large cooking apples, peeled, cored and thinly sliced (about 2⅓ cups)
- 1 box yellow cake mix with pudding
- 1¼ cups water
- ⅓ cup vegetable oil
- 3 eggs
- ¼ teaspoon apple pie spice

TOPPING

- ⅔ cup fluffy white whipped ready-to-spread frosting (from 12-oz container)
- ½ cup frozen (thawed) whipped topping
- Caramel topping, if desired

1 Heat oven to 350°F. In 1-quart saucepan, cook butter, whipping cream and brown sugar over low heat, stirring occasionally, just until butter is melted. Pour into ungreased 13 x 9-inch pan. Sprinkle with pecans; arrange sliced apples on top.

2 In large bowl, beat cake mix, water, oil, eggs and apple pie spice with electric mixer on low speed until moistened, then on medium speed 2 minutes, scraping bowl occasionally. Carefully spoon batter over apple mixture.

3 Bake 41 to 47 minutes or until toothpick inserted near center comes out clean. Cool 10 minutes. Run knife around sides of pan to loosen cake. Place heatproof serving platter upside down over pan; carefully turn platter and pan over. Leave pan over cake about 1 minute so caramel can drizzle over cake. Remove pan.

4 In small bowl, mix frosting and whipped topping. Serve warm cake topped with frosting mixture and drizzled with caramel topping. Store covered in refrigerator.

1 Serving: Calories 380; Total Fat 19g (Saturated Fat 8g, Trans Fat 1g); Cholesterol 65mg; Sodium 280mg; Total Carbohydrate 49g (Dietary Fiber 1g); Protein 2g **Exchanges:** ½ Starch, 3 Other Carbohydrate, 3½ Fat **Carbohydrate Choices:** 3

Sweet Secret You can use cinnamon in place of the apple pie spice for a slightly different flavor.

Sweet Secret Not a fan of whipped topping? You can use sweetened whipped cream from an aerosol can or make your own (page 6).

Banana-Nut Cake

16 servings | **PREP TIME: 15 Minutes** | **START TO FINISH: 2 Hours 5 Minutes**

CAKE

2⅓	cups all-purpose flour
1⅔	cups granulated sugar
1¼	cups mashed very ripe bananas (3 large)
⅔	cup shortening
⅔	cup finely chopped nuts
⅔	cup buttermilk
1¼	teaspoons baking powder
1¼	teaspoons baking soda
¾	teaspoon salt
3	eggs

CREAMY PEANUT BUTTER FROSTING

3	cups powdered sugar
⅓	cup peanut butter
1½	teaspoons vanilla, if desired
¼ to ⅓	cup milk

1 Heat oven to 350°F. Grease 13 × 9-inch pan with shortening; lightly flour.

2 In large bowl, beat cake ingredients with electric mixer on low speed 30 seconds, scraping bowl constantly. Beat on high speed 3 minutes, scraping bowl occasionally. Pour into pan.

3 Bake 45 to 50 minutes, or until toothpick inserted in center comes out clean. Cool on cooling rack. Cool completely, about 1 hour.

4 In medium bowl, mix powdered sugar and peanut butter with spoon or electric mixer on low speed. Stir in vanilla and ¼ cup milk. Beat until smooth and spreadable. If necessary, stir in additional milk, ½ teaspoon at a time. Spread frosting over cake.

1 Serving: Calories 420; Total Fat 16g (Saturated Fat 3.5g, Trans Fat 0g); Cholesterol 35mg; Sodium 300mg; Total Carbohydrate 64g (Dietary Fiber 1g); Protein 5g **Exchanges:** 1½ Starch, 3 Other Carbohydrate, 3 Fat **Carbohydrate Choices:** 4

Sweet Secret Use the pulse feature on your food processor to finely chop nuts. Or seal chopped nuts in a resealable food-storage plastic bag, and use a rolling pin to crush them.

Sweet Secret Too many overly ripe bananas? Simply peel bananas, wrap tightly in plastic wrap and freeze. Thaw the amount you need for recipes, such as this one!

Easy Banana Bread Coffee Cake

12 servings | **PREP TIME: 15 Minutes** | **START TO FINISH: 1 Hour 10 Minutes**

COFFEE CAKE

2 to 3	large ripe bananas, mashed (about 1⅓ cups)
⅔	cup granulated sugar
¼	cup milk
3	tablespoons vegetable oil
1	teaspoon ground cinnamon
3	eggs
2⅔	cups Original Bisquick™ mix
¾	cup chopped walnuts or pecans
1	large banana, sliced

STREUSEL

1	cup Original Bisquick mix
½	cup chopped walnuts or pecans
½	cup packed brown sugar
6	tablespoons butter, cut into small pieces

SERVE-WITH, IF DESIRED

Real maple or maple-flavored syrup

1 Heat oven to 350°F. Grease 13 × 9-inch pan with shortening or spray with cooking spray.

2 In large bowl, stir mashed bananas, granulated sugar, milk, oil, cinnamon and eggs. Stir in 2⅔ cups Bisquick mix and ¾ cup walnuts. Fold in sliced banana. Pour mixture into pan. In medium bowl, mix streusel ingredients, cutting in butter with pastry blender or fork until crumbly. Sprinkle over mixture in pan.

3 Bake 30 to 36 minutes or until knife inserted in center comes out clean. Cool 15 minutes. Cut into 4 rows by 3 rows. Serve warm with syrup. Store remaining coffee cake covered up to 3 days.

1 Serving: Calories 460; Total Fat 24g (Saturated Fat 7g, Trans Fat 1g); Cholesterol 60mg; Sodium 520mg; Total Carbohydrate 54g (Dietary Fiber 2g); Protein 6g **Exchanges:** 2 Starch, 1½ Other Carbohydrate, 4½ Fat **Carbohydrate Choices:** 3½

Sweet Secret Make this cake ahead, ready to bake when you are. Make as directed through step 2. Cover and refrigerate up to 12 hours. Uncover and bake as directed in step 3.

Banana Split Chocolate Mug Cake

1 mug cake | **PREP TIME: 5 Minutes** | **START TO FINISH: 15 Minutes**

¼ cup all-purpose flour

2 tablespoons sugar

2 tablespoons unsweetened baking cocoa

½ teaspoon baking powder

⅛ teaspoon salt

⅓ cup mashed banana (about 1 small)

3 tablespoons milk

1 tablespoon butter, melted

⅓ cup vanilla or favorite flavor ice cream

1 tablespoon hot fudge sauce

1 fresh strawberry

1 In small mixing bowl, mix flour, sugar, cocoa, baking powder and salt; stir with whisk until well blended. Add banana, milk and butter until smooth. Pour into a 10-oz microwavable mug.

2 Microwave on High 1 to 2 minutes or until set and cake rises (center will have a slightly wet appearance). Cool 5 minutes. Top with ice cream, hot fudge and the strawberry.

1 Mug Cake: Calories 620; Total Fat 21g (Saturated Fat 13g, Trans Fat 0.5g); Cholesterol 55mg; Sodium 770mg; Total Carbohydrate 98g (Dietary Fiber 7g); Protein 10g **Exchanges:** ½ Starch, ½ Fruit, 4½ Other Carbohydrate, 1 Milk, 2½ Fat **Carbohydrate Choices:** 6½

Simple Sparkle
Just for fun, add other toppings such as caramel ice-cream topping, whipped cream and chopped nuts.

Whole-Grain Banana-Almond Cake

9 servings | PREP TIME: 15 Minutes | START TO FINISH: 45 Minutes

CAKE

- ⅔ cup sliced almonds
- ⅓ cup old-fashioned or quick-cooking oats
- ⅓ cup all-purpose flour
- ⅓ cup whole wheat flour
- 1 teaspoon baking soda
- 1 teaspoon apple pie or pumpkin pie spice
- ¼ teaspoon salt
- ⅔ cup buttermilk
- ½ cup packed brown sugar
- ⅓ cup vegetable oil
- 1 teaspoon vanilla
- 1 egg
- 2 medium bananas, cut lengthwise in half

TOPPING

Maple-flavored or pure maple syrup, if desired

1 Heat oven to 350° F. Grease 8- or 9-inch square pan with shortening or spray with cooking spray.

2 In bowl of food processor, pulse ⅓ cup of the almonds until coarsely ground. Add oats; process until very finely ground. Transfer to medium bowl; stir in all-purpose flour, wheat flour, baking soda, pie spice and salt.

3 In large bowl, mix buttermilk, brown sugar, oil, vanilla and egg with whisk until blended. Stir in flour mixture until well blended. Pour into prepared pan. Place banana halves, cut side up, over batter; sprinkle with remaining almonds.

4 Bake 25 to 30 minutes or until toothpick inserted in center comes out clean. Serve warm or cool.

5 To serve, drizzle with maple syrup.

1 Serving: Calories 250; Total Fat 13g (Saturated Fat 2g, Trans Fat 0g); Cholesterol 20mg; Sodium 240mg; Total Carbohydrate 29g (Dietary Fiber 2g); Protein 4g **Exchanges:** 1 Starch, 1 Other Carbohydrate, 2½ Fat **Carbohydrate Choices:** 2

Sweet Secret Look for bananas that are about 8 inches long so they fit nicely in the pan.

Streusel-Topped Banana-Chocolate Snack Cake

12 servings | **PREP TIME: 15 Minutes** | **START TO FINISH: 2 Hours 5 Minutes**

CAKE

1½	cups Original Bisquick mix
½	cup whole wheat flour
½	cup packed brown sugar
2	ripe medium bananas, mashed (about 1 cup)
½	cup milk
1	teaspoon vanilla
½	cup semisweet chocolate chips

STREUSEL TOPPING

¼	cup packed brown sugar
¼	cup whole wheat flour
¼	teaspoon ground cinnamon
2	tablespoons cold butter

1 Heat oven to 425°F. Grease bottom and sides of 9-inch square pan with shortening or spray with cooking spray.

2 In large bowl, stir Bisquick mix, ½ cup flour, ½ cup brown sugar, the bananas, milk and vanilla. Gently fold in chocolate chips. Pour into pan.

3 In medium bowl, mix ¼ cup brown sugar, ¼ cup flour and the cinnamon. Cut in butter, using pastry blender (or pulling 2 table knives through ingredients in opposite directions), until mixture is crumbly. Sprinkle topping evenly over batter in pan.

4 Bake 17 to 20 minutes or until toothpick inserted in center comes out clean. Cool completely on cooling rack, about 1 hour 30 minutes.

1 Serving: Calories 110; Total Fat 3g (Saturated Fat 1.5g, Trans Fat 0g); Cholesterol 0mg; Sodium 105mg; Total Carbohydrate 19g (Dietary Fiber 1g); Protein 1g **Exchanges:** ½ Starch, 1 Other Carbohydrate, ½ Fat **Carbohydrate Choices:** 1

Sweet Secret For a more rustic version, use chocolate chunks or chopped chocolate bars instead of chips.

Sweet Secret Cut into smaller squares for party-size bites.

Gooey Caramel-Banana Trifle

6 servings | PREP TIME: 25 Minutes | START TO FINISH: 2 Hours 45 Minutes

1 box white angel food cake mix

1¼ cups water

1 box (6-serving size) vanilla pudding and pie filling mix (not instant)

3 cups milk

3 cups Sweetened Whipped Cream (page 6)

½ cup sour cream

1 can (13.4 oz) dulce de leche (caramelized sweetened condensed milk)

3 medium bananas, sliced (about 3 cups)

1 Heat oven to 350°F. Make and bake cake mix as directed on box for 10-inch angel food (tube) cake pan, using 1¼ cups water. Cool completely, about 1 hour.

2 Meanwhile, in 2-quart saucepan, cook pudding mix and 3 cups milk as directed on box. Cool 20 minutes. Fold whipped cream and sour cream into pudding.

3 Cut or tear cake into 1-inch cubes. In small microwavable bowl, microwave dulce de leche uncovered on High 30 seconds; stir. In 3-quart glass bowl or trifle bowl, arrange one-third of the cake cubes. Top with one-third of the pudding mixture, one-third of the sliced bananas and one-third of the dulce de leche. Repeat layers twice.

4 Cover; refrigerate at least 1 hour but no longer than 24 hours. Just before serving, top with additional whipped cream and banana slices if desired. Store covered in refrigerator.

1 Serving: Calories 250; Total Fat 5g (Saturated Fat 4g, Trans Fat 0g); Cholesterol 0mg; Sodium 290mg; Total Carbohydrate 44g (Dietary Fiber 0g); Protein 4g **Exchanges:** ½ Fruit, 2 Other Carbohydrate, ½ Milk **Carbohydrate Choices:** 3

Sweet Secret If you like, substitute 1 container (8 ounces) frozen whipped topping, thawed, for the Sweetened Whipped Cream.

Sweet Secret Make it even faster by purchasing an angel food cake from your grocery store bakery. If a tube-shaped cake isn't available, two loaf-shaped cakes will work instead.

Caramelized Banana Cake with Salted Caramel Glaze

12 servings | **PREP TIME: 20 Minutes** | **START TO FINISH: 2 Hours 20 Minutes**

CAKE

- 2 tablespoons butter, melted
- 2 tablespoons packed brown sugar
- 2 sliced ripe medium bananas
- 1 box spice cake mix with pudding
- 1 cup sour cream
- ¾ cup vegetable oil
- 4 eggs
- 1 cup chopped walnuts, toasted

GLAZE

- ⅓ cup caramel topping
- Kosher salt

1 Heat oven to 325°F. Grease 10- or 12-cup fluted tube cake pan with shortening; lightly flour.

2 In large microwavable bowl, mix butter, brown sugar and bananas. Microwave uncovered on High 1 minute 40 seconds to 2 minutes or until bananas are cooked and caramelized.

3 Add cake mix, sour cream, vegetable oil and eggs. Beat with electric mixer on low speed 1 minute. Increase speed to medium; beat 2 minutes. Stir in walnuts. Pour into pan.

4 Bake 40 to 45 minutes or until toothpick inserted in center comes out clean. Cool 15 minutes. Turn upside down onto cooling rack or heatproof serving plate; remove pan. Cool completely, about 1 hour. Place cake on serving plate.

5 Drizzle cake with caramel topping. Sprinkle with kosher salt.

1 Serving: Calories 340; Total Fat 28g (Saturated Fat 7g, Trans Fat 0g); Cholesterol 75mg; Sodium 400mg; Total Carbohydrate 18g (Dietary Fiber 1g); Protein 4g **Exchanges:** 1 Starch, 5½ Fat **Carbohydrate Choices:** 1

Sweet Secret Can't find spice cake mix? Substitute yellow cake mix and 1 teaspoon pumpkin pie spice instead.

Sweet Secret To toast walnuts, sprinkle in ungreased heavy skillet. Cook over medium heat 5 to 7 minutes, stirring frequently until walnuts begin to brown, then stirring constantly until walnuts are light brown.

Sweet Secret This cake was photographed using a specialty fluted tube cake pan. Deeper pans like the heritage pan may require an additional 2 to 7 minutes of bake time.

Upside-Down Poppy Seed-Pear Cake

12 servings | PREP TIME: 10 Minutes | START TO FINISH: 1 Hour

½   cup butter

⅔   cup packed brown sugar

3   medium pears, peeled, cut into ¼-inch slices

1   cup sliced almonds

1   box pound cake mix

⅔   cup milk

¼   cup butter

2   eggs

2   tablespoons poppy seed filling (from 12½-oz can)

⅓   cup sliced almonds, toasted

1 Heat oven to 350°F. Spray 13 × 9-inch pan with cooking spray; add ½ cup butter. Melt butter in oven 5 minutes. Stir in brown sugar until well mixed; spread evenly in pan. Arrange pear slices over sugar mixture; sprinkle with 1 cup almonds.

2 Make cake mix as directed on box, using milk, ¼ cup butter and eggs. Fold in poppy seed filling. Spoon batter over pears in pan.

3 Bake 30 to 35 minutes or until golden brown and toothpick inserted in center comes out clean. Run knife around sides of pan to loosen cake. Place heatproof serving plate or foil-lined cookie sheet upside down on pan; turn plate and pan over. Leave pan over cake 1 minute to allow topping to drizzle over cake; remove pan. Cool 10 minutes. Sprinkle with toasted almonds.

1 Serving: Calories 390; Total Fat 19g (Saturated Fat 9g, Trans Fat 0g); Cholesterol 0mg; Sodium 260mg; Total Carbohydrate 55g (Dietary Fiber 2g); Protein 5g **Exchanges:** 1 Starch, ½ Fruit, 2 Other Carbohydrate, 3½ Fat **Carbohydrate Choices:** 3½

Simple Sparkle Serve this cake warm with a scoop of ice cream so it will melt into the cake.

Easy Pear-Ginger Dump Cake

12 servings | **PREP TIME: 15 Minutes** | **START TO FINISH: 55 Minutes**

6 cups (peeled if desired) chopped ripe pears (3 to 4 pears)

2 tablespoons finely chopped crystallized ginger

2 cups Easy Scratch Cake Mix (page 7)

¾ cup butter, melted

½ cup salted caramel or caramel topping

½ cup pecan halves

Vanilla ice cream, if desired

1 Heat oven to 350°F. Grease bottom and sides of 13 × 9-inch pan with shortening or spray with cooking spray. Spread pears in bottom of pan; sprinkle with crystallized ginger.

2 Sprinkle cake mix evenly over pears. Use back of spoon to smooth cake mix. Drizzle with melted butter and caramel topping; sprinkle with pecans.

3 Bake 35 to 40 minutes or until pears are tender. Serve warm with ice cream.

1 Serving: Calories 310; Total Fat 16g (Saturated Fat 8g, Trans Fat 0g); Cholesterol 35mg; Sodium 230mg; Total Carbohydrate 41g (Dietary Fiber 2g); Protein 2g **Exchanges:** 1 Starch, 1½ Other Carbohydrate, 3 Fat **Carbohydrate Choices:** 3

Sweet Secret You can use any type of pear in this homespun dessert, but make sure they are ripe.

Sweet Secret Unripe pears? Place them in a lunch-size paper bag with an apple. Close the bag and leave it on the counter for a few days. The apple will help the pears ripen faster.

Sweet Secret You can substitute ½ package yellow or white cake mix with pudding (dry) for the Easy Scratch Cake Mix (about 1½ cups).

Dried Pear–Hazelnut Loaf

16 servings | **PREP TIME: 20 Minutes** | **START TO FINISH: 3 Hours 45 Minutes**

2¼ cups all-purpose flour

1 cup granulated sugar

2 teaspoons baking powder

½ teaspoon salt

1 cup buttermilk

6 tablespoons butter, melted

1 teaspoon vanilla

1 teaspoon grated lemon peel

1 teaspoon grated gingerroot

2 eggs

¾ cup chopped dried pears

½ cup chopped hazelnuts (filberts), toasted, skins removed

½ cup packed brown sugar

¼ cup cold butter

⅔ cup all-purpose flour

½ cup powdered sugar

2 teaspoons milk

1. Heat oven to 375°F. Spray bottom and sides of 9 × 5-inch loaf pan with cooking spray.

2. In large bowl, mix 2¼ cups flour, the granulated sugar, baking powder and salt. In medium bowl, beat buttermilk, 6 tablespoons butter, the vanilla, lemon peel, gingerroot and eggs with whisk until well blended. Stir into flour mixture until blended. Stir in pears and hazelnuts. Spread batter in pan.

3. In medium bowl, mix brown sugar and ¼ cup butter until blended. Stir in ⅔ cup flour; pinch with fingers until clumps form. Sprinkle topping over batter.

4. Bake 1 hour to 1 hour 5 minutes or until toothpick inserted in center comes out clean, covering with foil during last 25 minutes to prevent overbrowning if necessary. Cool 10 minutes; remove from pan to cooling rack. Cool completely, about 2 hours.

5. In small bowl, mix powdered sugar and milk until thin enough to drizzle. Drizzle over loaf. Let stand 10 minutes.

1 Serving: Calories 300; Total Fat 11g (Saturated Fat 5g, Trans Fat 0g); Cholesterol 0mg; Sodium 230mg; Total Carbohydrate 48g (Dietary Fiber 1g); Protein 4g **Exchanges:** 1 Starch, ½ Fruit, 1½ Other Carbohydrate, 2 Fat **Carbohydrate Choices:** 3

Sweet Secret To toast hazelnuts, sprinkle in ungreased heavy skillet. Cook over medium heat 5 to 7 minutes, stirring frequently until hazelnuts begin to brown, then stirring constantly until hazelnuts are light brown.

Lemon-Pear Gingerbread Trifle

12 servings | **PREP TIME: 20 Minutes** | **START TO FINISH: 13 Hours 55 Minutes**

1 box gingerbread cake and cookie mix

1¼ cups lukewarm water

1 egg

2 cans (15 oz each) sliced pears

1 can (15.75 oz) lemon pie filling

2 cups whipping cream

1 Heat oven to 350°F. Spray bottom only of 13 × 9-inch pan with cooking spray.

2 In large bowl, stir gingerbread mix, water and egg with fork until blended. Stir vigorously about 2 minutes until well mixed. Pour into pan.

3 Bake 18 to 20 minutes or until toothpick inserted in center comes out clean.

4 Meanwhile, drain pears into 2-cup glass measuring cup, reserving ¾ cup liquid. Add ½ cup of the pie filling to pear liquid. Microwave uncovered on High 1 to 2 minutes or until heated; stir with whisk until smooth. Refrigerate pears and remaining pie filling.

5 Poke top of warm cake in several places with fork. Pour warm lemon sauce over cake; spread evenly. Cool completely, about 1 hour.

6 Cut cake into 1½-inch squares. In large bowl, beat whipping cream with electric mixer on high speed until thickened. Gradually beat in remaining pie filling; continue beating until thickened. Place one-third of the cake cubes in bottom of 2-quart clear glass bowl. Spread with one-third of the cream mixture. Arrange one-third of the pears on cream mixture. Repeat layers twice with cake, cream mixture and pears. Cover; refrigerate at least 12 hours.

1 Serving: Calories 370; Total Fat 17g (Saturated Fat 9g, Trans Fat 0g); Cholesterol 60mg; Sodium 250mg; Total Carbohydrate 51g (Dietary Fiber 1g); Protein 3g **Exchanges:** 1 Starch, 2½ Other Carbohydrate, 3 Fat **Carbohydrate Choices:** 3½

Sweet Secret For a smaller trifle, cut only half of the gingerbread into pieces and use half the amount of pears, lemon filling and whipping cream. Freeze the remaining gingerbread.

Simple Sparkle Sprinkle a little chopped crystallized ginger over the trifle.

Easy Lemon Loaf

12 servings | **PREP TIME: 10 Minutes** | **START TO FINISH: 2 Hours 10 Minutes**

1 box white cake mix with pudding

2 containers (6 oz each) lemon burst yogurt

½ cup butter, melted

1 tablespoon grated lemon peel

2 eggs

2 teaspoons coarse sugar, if desired

1 Heat oven to 350°F. Grease 9 × 5-inch loaf pan with shortening; lightly flour.

2 In large bowl, beat cake mix, yogurt, melted butter, lemon peel and eggs with electric mixer on low speed until ingredients are moistened; scrape bottom and side of bowl. Beat 2 minutes on medium speed. Pour batter into pan. Sprinkle with coarse sugar.

3 Bake 40 to 50 minutes or until toothpick inserted in center of loaf comes out clean. Cool in pan on cooling rack 10 minutes. Run knife around sides of pan to loosen loaf. Remove from pan to cooling rack. Cool completely, about 1 hour.

1 Serving: Calories 91; Total Fat 9g (Saturated Fat 5g, Trans Fat 0g); Cholesterol 51mg; Sodium 14mg; Total Carbohydrate 4g (Dietary Fiber 1g); Protein 1g **Exchanges:** 1 Starch, 1½ Other Carbohydrate, 2 Fat **Carbohydrate Choices:** 2

Simple Sparkle Top this loaf cake with a glaze. Mix 1 cup powdered sugar and 2 teaspoons milk until smooth. Drizzle over loaf, and let glaze set before slicing.

Simple Sparkle Serve slices of this loaf cake with whipped cream and fresh berries.

Lemonade-Coconut Icebox Cake

12 servings | **PREP TIME: 20 Minutes** | **START TO FINISH: 12 Hours 20 Minutes**

1 box (4-serving size) coconut cream instant pudding and pie filling mix

1¾ cups milk

¾ cup heavy whipping cream

½ cup frozen lemonade concentrate (from 12-oz can), thawed

1 package (8 oz) cream cheese, softened

3 cups crumbled coconut macaroon cookies (from 9 oz package)

½ cup coconut, toasted

1 In medium bowl, prepare pudding mix with milk as directed on box; set aside.

2 In large bowl, beat whipping cream, lemonade concentrate and cream cheese with electric mixer on low speed 1 minute or until blended and mixture begins to thicken. Gradually increase speed to high, beating just until stiff peaks form.

3 Press crumbled cookies in bottom of 9-inch springform pan, pressing gently to cover the bottom of the pan. Spread whipped cream mixture evenly over cookies. Spread pudding over the whipped cream mixture. Sprinkle evenly with toasted coconut. Cover with plastic wrap; refrigerate at least 12 hours but no longer than 48 hours.

4 To serve, run knife around side of pan to loosen cake. Remove side of pan. Place cake on serving plate; cut into wedges.

1 Serving: Calories 550; Total Fat 29g (Saturated Fat 22g, Trans Fat 0g); Cholesterol 45mg; Sodium 350mg; Total Carbohydrate 68g (Dietary Fiber 4g); Protein 4g **Exchanges:** 1½ Starch, 3 Other Carbohydrate, 5½ Fat **Carbohydrate Choices:** 4½

Sweet Secret Perfect for a summer day, this icebox cake can also be frozen and served icy cold. Prepare as directed and freeze overnight. Let stand at room temperature 15 minutes before serving.

Lemon–Cream Cheese Bundt Cake with Lemon Glaze

12 servings | PREP TIME: 10 Minutes | START TO FINISH: 2 Hours 10 Minutes

CAKE

- 1 box yellow cake mix with pudding
- 1 cup milk
- 1 package (3 oz) cream cheese, softened
- 2 tablespoons grated lemon peel
- ¼ cup lemon juice
- 3 eggs

GLAZE

- 2 cups powdered sugar
- 2 tablespoons lemon juice

1 Heat oven to 325°F. Grease 10- or 12-cup fluted tube cake pan with shortening; lightly flour.

2 In large bowl, beat cake ingredients with electric mixer on low speed 1 minute, scraping bowl constantly. Increase speed to medium; beat 2 minutes. Pour into pan.

3 Bake 40 to 45 minutes or until toothpick inserted in center comes out clean. Cool 15 minutes. Turn upside down onto cooling rack or heatproof serving plate; remove pan. Cool completely, about 1 hour.

4 Place cake on serving plate. In medium bowl, beat powdered sugar and lemon juice, a little at a time, using whisk until thick glaze forms. (You may not need all the juice.) Pour evenly over cake. Store loosely covered.

1 Serving: Calories 270; Total Fat 5g (Saturated Fat 3g, Trans Fat 0g); Cholesterol 55mg; Sodium 310mg; Total Carbohydrate 52g (Dietary Fiber 0g); Protein 3g **Exchanges:** 1 Starch, 2½ Other Carbohydrate, 1 Fat **Carbohydrate Choices:** 3½

Sweet Secret Grate the lemon peel right into the bowl with the other ingredients to keep all those bright citrus flavors from drying out in the air.

Blackberry-Lemon Yogurt Trifle

20 servings | **PREP TIME: 20 Minutes** | **START TO FINISH: 20 Minutes**

3 containers (6 oz each) lemon meringue yogurt

2 cups Sweetened Whipped Cream (page 6) or frozen whipped topping, thawed

3 containers (6 oz each) blackberry yogurt

8 cups cubed (1-inch) angel food cake (12- to 15-oz cake)

4 cups fresh or frozen (thawed) blackberries

2 tablespoons grated lemon peel

1 In medium bowl, mix lemon meringue yogurt with 1 cup of the whipped cream. In another medium bowl, mix blackberry yogurt with remaining 1 cup whipped cream; set aside.

2 In 2- to 3-quart trifle bowl or clear glass bowl, arrange half of the cake cubes. Top with 2 cups of the blackberries. Top with blackberry yogurt mixture. Arrange remaining cake cubes over yogurt. Top with remaining blackberries. Spoon lemon yogurt mixture over berries. Sprinkle with lemon peel. Refrigerate until ready to serve. Cover and refrigerate any remaining trifle.

1 Serving: Calories 150; Total Fat 5g (Saturated Fat 3g, Trans Fat 0g); Cholesterol 20mg; Sodium 180mg; Total Carbohydrate 22g (Dietary Fiber 1g); Protein 3g **Exchanges:** 1 Starch, ½ Fruit, 1 Fat **Carbohydrate Choices:** 1½

Fabulous Cake Hacks

These terrific tips and tricks from the Betty Crocker Kitchens make it easy to bake great cakes every time.

OVEN KNOW-HOW

Ovens tend to lose accuracy over time. Be sure you're baking at the right temperature by investing in an inexpensive oven thermometer and placing it in the center of your oven. If it doesn't show the temperature you set the oven to, adjust the heat until the thermometer reads the correct temperature.

SHELL FREE

Keep egg shells from getting into the batter by breaking them, one at a time, into a custard cup or small bowl before adding to the batter.

SLIDE OUT

Spray liquid measuring cup with cooking spray before filling with sticky liquids like honey or corn syrup—they will slide right out.

SLICK TRICK

Use a pastry brush to easily brush shortening into pans and their crevices.

SOFTENING BROWN SUGAR

Place 1 to 3 cups hard brown sugar in microwavable bowl. Cover with damp paper towel, then plastic wrap. Microwave on High 1 minute. Let stand 2 minutes until softened. Repeat heating once or twice more if needed.

EASY OUT

Follow the directions in the recipe for cake cooling and pan removal. If a cake is left in the pan too long and is difficult to remove, try reheating the pan in the oven for a minute; then remove it from the pan.

FLIP, NOT FLOP

Keep cakes from falling apart when removing them from the pans by doing it in two steps:

1 Run knife around side of pan to loosen cake. Place cooling rack or upside-down plate on top of cake. Holding top and bottom with hands, invert cake, then remove pan.

2 Quickly place another cooling rack on top of upside-down cake. Invert again to get cake on a cooling rack, right-side up.

CAKE INGREDIENT SUBSTITUTIONS

Never make a last-minute dash to the store for a needed ingredient. Use this handy chart for easy substitutions.

FOOD/AMOUNT	REPLACE WITH
Baking powder, 1 teaspoon	½ teaspoon cream of tartar + ¼ teaspoon baking soda
Brown sugar, 1 cup	1 cup granulated sugar + 2 tablespoons molasses
Buttermilk, 1 cup	1 tablespoon lemon juice or white vinegar + enough milk to make 1 cup
Chocolate Unsweetened baking, 1 ounce Semisweet chips, 1 cup Semisweet baking, 1 ounce	3 tablespoons cocoa + 1 tablespoon melted shortening 6 ounces semisweet baking chocolate, chopped 1 ounce unsweetened baking chocolate + 1 tablespoon sugar OR 1 tablespoon cocoa + 2 tablespoons sugar and 2 teaspoons shortening

Soften butter stick by removing the wrapper and placing in a microwavable bowl. Microwave on Low (30%) 10 to 40 seconds or until butter is softened but not melted.

Lemon-Poppy Seed Poke Cake

12 servings | **PREP TIME: 20 Minutes** | **START TO FINISH: 2 Hours**

CAKE

- 1 box lemon cake mix with pudding
- 1 cup water
- ½ cup vegetable oil
- 3 eggs
- 2 tablespoons poppy seed

LEMON SYRUP

- ⅓ cup sugar
- ¼ cup freshly squeezed lemon juice

TOPPING

- 1 container fluffy white whipped ready-to-spread frosting
- 1 teaspoon grated lemon peel

1 Heat oven to 350°F. Grease or spray bottom only of 13 x 9-inch pan.

2 In large bowl, beat cake mix, water, oil and eggs with electric mixer on low speed 30 seconds, then on medium speed 2 minutes, scraping bowl occasionally. Stir in poppy seed. Pour into pan. Bake 26 to 33 minutes or until toothpick inserted in center comes out clean.

3 Meanwhile, in 1-quart saucepan, cook and stir sugar and lemon juice over medium heat about 3 minutes or until dissolved. Set aside.

4 Cool cake on cooling rack 5 minutes. With long-tined fork or toothpick, poke holes halfway down in cake every ½-inch. Drizzle lemon syrup over cake. Cool completely on cooling rack, about 1 hour.

5 Spread frosting evenly over cake. Sprinkle with lemon peel.

1 Serving: Calories 400; Total Fat 19g (Saturated Fat 6g, Trans Fat 0g); Cholesterol 45mg; Sodium 310mg; Total Carbohydrate 53g (Dietary Fiber 0g); Protein 2g **Exchanges:** 1 Starch, 2½ Other Carbohydrate, 3½ Fat **Carbohydrate Choices:** 3½

Sweet Secret This cake also works well with other citrus flavors such as orange and lime. Have fun experimenting!

Simple Sparkle Raspberries make a lovely garnish for this poke cake. Just include a few on each plate as you're serving.

Peaches and Vanilla Bean Bundt Cake

12 servings | **PREP TIME: 20 Minutes** | **START TO FINISH: 2 Hours 25 Minutes**

CAKE

- 1 box white cake mix with pudding
- 1 cup milk
- 3 oz cream cheese, softened
- 1½ teaspoons vanilla bean paste
- ¼ cup peach preserves
- 3 eggs
- 1 cup diced fresh peaches or diced frozen (thawed and drained) peaches

GLAZE

- 2 oz cream cheese, softened
- 3 tablespoons butter, softened
- 1 cup powdered sugar
- 1 tablespoon milk
- ½ teaspoon vanilla bean paste

1 Heat oven to 325°F. Grease 10- or 12-cup fluted tube cake pan with shortening; lightly flour.

2 In large bowl, beat all cake ingredients except peaches with electric mixer on low speed 1 minute, scraping bowl constantly. Increase speed to medium; beat 2 minutes. Pour into pan. Sprinkle peaches on top of cake batter.

3 Bake 45 to 50 minutes or until toothpick inserted in center comes out clean. Cool 15 minutes. Turn upside down onto cooling rack or heatproof serving plate; remove pan. Cool completely, about 1 hour. Place cake on serving plate.

4 In medium bowl, beat 2 oz cream cheese and the butter with electric mixer on medium speed until smooth. Beat in powdered sugar, 1 tablespoon milk and ½ teaspoon vanilla bean paste until smooth. Spread mixture on top of cooled cake.

1 Serving: Calories 310; Total Fat 10g (Saturated Fat 6g, Trans Fat 0g); Cholesterol 70mg; Sodium 360mg; Total Carbohydrate 48g (Dietary Fiber 0g); Protein 5g **Exchanges:** ½ Starch, 2½ Other Carbohydrate, ½ Low-Fat Milk, 1½ Fat **Carbohydrate Choices:** 3

Sweet Secret Vanilla bean paste is available at many grocery stores and superstores. If you prefer, substitute an equal amount of vanilla extract for the vanilla bean paste. Or, use half of a scraped-out vanilla bean.

Sweet Secret This cake was photographed using a specialty fluted tube cake pan. Deeper pans may require an additional 2 to 7 minutes of bake time.

Key Lime Magic Custard Cake

9 servings | **PREP TIME: 20 Minutes** | **START TO FINISH: 3 Hours 10 Minutes**

CAKE

- 4 eggs, separated
- 1 cup powdered sugar
- ½ cup butter, melted and cooled
- 1 tablespoon grated lime peel
- 3 tablespoons Key lime juice or lime juice
- 1 cup all-purpose flour
- 1 cup whole milk
- 1 can (14 oz) sweetened condensed milk (not evaporated)

GARNISH

Sweetened Whipped Cream (page 6) or frozen whipped topping, thawed, if desired

Grated lime peel, if desired

1 Heat oven to 325°F. Grease bottom and sides of 9-inch square pan with shortening or spray with cooking spray.

2 In medium bowl, beat egg whites with electric mixer on high speed about 2 minutes or until stiff peaks form. Set aside.

3 In large bowl, beat egg yolks and powdered sugar with electric mixer on medium speed about 5 minutes, scraping bowl occasionally, or until pale and smooth. Add butter, 1 tablespoon lime peel and the lime juice; beat until well blended. Add flour; beat just until flour is moistened (mixture will be very thick).

4 With mixer on low speed, gradually add milk and condensed milk; mix until smooth. Gently fold in egg whites. Mixture may appear slightly curdled. Pour into pan.

5 Bake 45 to 50 minutes or just until center is set. Cool completely, about 2 hours. Cover and refrigerate until ready to serve but no longer than 24 hours. To serve, top with Sweetened Whipped Cream and lime peel.

1 Serving: Calories 390; Total Fat 17g (Saturated Fat 10g, Trans Fat 0.5g); Cholesterol 130mg; Sodium 180mg; Total Carbohydrate 50g (Dietary Fiber 0g); Protein 8g **Exchanges:** 2½ Starch, 1 Other Carbohydrate, 3 Fat **Carbohydrate Choices:** 3

Sweet Secret Be sure you use a 9-inch square pan. Due to the volume, an 8-inch square pan won't work for this recipe.

Sweet Secret Key limes are smaller and more tart and aromatic than the regular Persian limes common in the grocery store. Both Key lime juice and regular lime juice come bottled, but for the best flavor, use fresh juice if possible.

Cranberry Trifle Squares

12 servings | **PREP TIME: 20 Minutes** | **START TO FINISH: 2 Hours 35 Minutes**

2 cups sugar

1½ cups water

1 bag (12 oz) fresh or frozen cranberries

½ teaspoon almond extract

2 cups heavy whipping cream

¼ cup sugar

1 package (10.75 oz) frozen pound cake loaf, thawed, cut into 10 slices

1 cup crushed sugar cookies

⅓ cup sliced almonds

1 In 2-quart saucepan, heat 2 cups sugar and the water to boiling over high heat, stirring occasionally. Boil 10 minutes. Stir in cranberries; reduce heat to medium-high. Cook uncovered 3 to 4 minutes or until all cranberries have popped. Stir in almond extract; cool.

2 In chilled large bowl, beat whipping cream and ¼ cup sugar on high speed until stiff peaks form.

3 In 11 × 7-inch (2-quart) glass baking dish, arrange cake slices, cutting slices if necessary, to cover bottom of dish. Spoon cranberry sauce over cake. Sprinkle with sugar cookies. Spread whipped cream over sugar cookies. Sprinkle with almonds.

4 Cover and refrigerate at least 2 or up to 24 hours before serving. Cut into squares. Store covered in refrigerator.

1 Serving: Calories 480; Total Fat 24g (Saturated Fat 12g, Trans Fat 1g); Cholesterol 80mg; Sodium 95mg; Total Carbohydrate 64g (Dietary Fiber 2g); Protein 4g **Exchanges:** 1 Starch, ½ Fruit, 2½ Other Carbohydrate, 4½ Fat **Carbohydrate Choices:** 4

Sweet Secret Want to enjoy this dessert year-round? Stock up on fresh cranberries when they're on sale in the fall and winter, and store them refrigerated or frozen. Refrigerate these tart red berries for up to 2 months or freeze up to 1 year.

Cranberry-Orange Pound Cake

16 servings | **PREP TIME: 20 Minutes** | **START TO FINISH: 2 Hours 40 Minutes**

CAKE

- 1 box golden vanilla or yellow cake mix with pudding
- 1 box (4-serving size) vanilla instant pudding and pie filling mix
- 1 cup water
- ½ cup butter, softened
- 1 to 2 teaspoons grated orange peel
- 4 eggs
- 1½ cups fresh or frozen cranberries, chopped (do not thaw frozen cranberries)
- Powdered sugar, if desired

ORANGE SAUCE, IF DESIRED

- 1 cup granulated sugar
- 1 tablespoon all-purpose flour
- ½ cup orange juice
- ½ cup butter

1 Heat oven to 325°F. Grease 12-cup fluted tube cake pan with shortening; lightly flour.

2 In large bowl, beat cake mix, pudding mix, water, softened butter, orange peel and eggs with electric mixer on low speed 30 seconds, scraping bowl constantly, then on medium speed 2 minutes, scraping bowl occasionally. Fold in cranberries. Spread in pan.

3 Bake 57 to 65 minutes or until toothpick inserted in center comes out clean. Cool 15 minutes. Place heatproof plate upside down over pan; turn plate and pan over; remove pan. Cool completely, about 1 hour. Sprinkle with powdered sugar.

4 In 1-quart saucepan, cook sauce ingredients over medium heat about 4 minutes, stirring constantly, until thickened and bubbly. Serve warm or cool sauce with cake. Store cake loosely covered at room temperature and sauce covered in refrigerator.

1 Serving: Calories 200; Total Fat 8g (Saturated Fat 4.5g, Trans Fat 0g); Cholesterol 70mg; Sodium 340mg; Total Carbohydrate 30g (Dietary Fiber 0g); Protein 2g **Exchanges:** 1 Starch, 1 Other Carbohydrate, 1½ Fat **Carbohydrate Choices:** 2

Sweet Secret This moist and fruity cake can be frozen up to 2 months.

Sweet Secret Bake this fresh cranberry cake in a kugelhopf pan for a fancier look. You can find this fluted pan in specialty cookware stores.

Fresh Fruit "Cake"

8 servings | **PREP TIME: 30 Minutes** | **START TO FINISH: 1 Hour 30 Minutes**

1 container (8 oz) mascarpone cheese

¾ cup heavy whipping cream

1 tablespoon sugar

2 teaspoons grated orange peel

3 slices (½-inch thick) watermelon (9- to 10-inch diameter), rind removed

1 cup blueberries

1 cup sliced strawberries

3 kiwifruit, peeled, sliced

6 to 8 wooden skewers

1 In large bowl, beat mascarpone cheese, whipping cream, sugar and 2 teaspoons orange peel with electric mixer on low speed until mixture begins to thicken. Gradually increase speed to high and beat 2 to 3 minutes, scraping bowl constantly, or until soft peaks form. Reserve ½ cup of the mascarpone mixture; set aside.

2 Place 1 slice of watermelon on serving plate. Spread about ¾ cup of the mascarpone mixture over watermelon; arrange blueberries on top, pressing slightly to adhere to mascarpone mixture. Arrange strawberry slices on top of blueberries.

3 Place another slice of watermelon on top; spread about ¾ cup mascarpone mixture over watermelon slice. Arrange kiwi slices on top, pressing slightly to adhere to mascarpone mixture. Top with remaining watermelon slice. Drop remaining mascarpone mixture by spoonfuls onto top of cake. Refrigerate uncovered at least 1 hour or until set but no longer than 48 hours.

4 When ready to serve, insert wooden skewers through top of cake to secure the layers. Cut into wedges; place on serving plates. Serve immediately. Remove skewers before eating.

1 Serving: Calories 270; Total Fat 22g (Saturated Fat 13g, Trans Fat 1g); Cholesterol 65mg; Sodium 25mg; Total Carbohydrate 16g (Dietary Fiber 2g); Protein 2g **Exchanges:** ½ Starch, ½ Fruit, 4½ Fat **Carbohydrate Choices:** 1

Sweet Secret You will need a large watermelon with a diameter of 9 to 10 inches to cut 8 good-size wedges for this cake.

Sweet Secret To make it easier to cut the 3 slices from the watermelon, first cut out a 1½-inch-diameter piece from the center of the watermelon and cut off the rind. Then cut horizontally into 3 slices.

Sweet Secret If you wish, build the cake in a springform pan to help hold the layers together and upright. Remove the side of the pan before slicing.

Ginger-Orange Pound Cake

16 servings | **PREP TIME: 25 Minutes** | **START TO FINISH: 3 Hours 10 Minutes**

CAKE

3	cups all-purpose flour
1	teaspoon baking powder
¼	teaspoon salt
2	tablespoons grated gingerroot
1	tablespoon grated orange peel
2	cups sugar
1½	cups butter, softened
5	eggs
1	cup orange juice

TOPPING

½	cup orange marmalade
¼	cup chopped candied ginger

1 Heat oven to 325°F. Grease 12-cup fluted tube pan with shortening; lightly flour. (Do not use dark or nonstick pan.)

2 In large bowl, mix flour, baking powder, salt, gingerroot and orange peel; set aside.

3 In another large bowl, beat sugar and butter with electric mixer on low speed 30 seconds, scraping bowl constantly, until creamy. Add eggs and beat until well blended. Beat on high speed 5 minutes, scraping bowl occasionally. Beat in flour mixture alternately with orange juice on low speed until smooth. Pour into pan.

4 Bake 1 hour 5 minutes to 1 hour 15 minutes or until toothpick inserted in center comes out clean and top is dark golden brown. Cool 30 minutes; remove from pan to cooling rack. Cool completely, about 1 hour.

5 Spoon marmalade over cake; top with candied ginger.

1 Serving: Calories 400; Total Fat 19g (Saturated Fat 11g, Trans Fat 1g); Cholesterol 110mg; Sodium 210mg; Total Carbohydrate 53g (Dietary Fiber 0g); Protein 5g **Exchanges:** 1 Starch, 2½ Other Carbohydrate, 3½ Fat **Carbohydrate Choices:** 3½

Sweet Secret Use a sharp, fine-mesh grater to grate fresh gingerroot. Discard the fibers that are left on the grater.

Simple Sparkle Garnish the cake with sugared kumquats. To sugar the kumquats, brush with corn syrup and roll in granulated sugar.

Blueberry-Orange Cornmeal Cake

8 servings | **PREP TIME: 15 Minutes** | **START TO FINISH: 1 Hour**

CAKE

- ⅔ cup milk
- ½ cup granulated sugar
- ½ cup olive oil
- 2 teaspoons grated orange peel
- 1 teaspoon vanilla
- 2 eggs
- 1¼ cups all-purpose flour
- ½ cup yellow cornmeal
- 2½ teaspoons baking powder
- ½ teaspoon salt
- ¾ cup fresh or frozen blueberries

GARNISH

- Powdered sugar, if desired

1 Heat oven to 350°F. Line bottom of 9-inch round pan with parchment paper. Grease side of pan with shortening or spray with cooking spray.

2 In medium bowl, mix milk, sugar, oil, orange peel, vanilla and eggs with whisk until blended. Add flour, cornmeal, baking powder and salt. Mix with whisk until smooth. Pour into pan; sprinkle with blueberries.

3 Bake 25 to 30 minutes or until toothpick inserted in center comes out clean. Cool 10 minutes. Remove from pan to cooling rack. Serve warm or at room temperature, sprinkled with powdered sugar.

1 Serving: Calories 320; Total Fat 16g (Saturated Fat 2.5g, Trans Fat 0g); Cholesterol 50mg; Sodium 330mg; Total Carbohydrate 39g (Dietary Fiber 1g); Protein 5g **Exchanges:** 2 Starch, ½ Other Carbohydrate, 3 Fat **Carbohydrate Choices:** 2½

Sweet Secret When whisking the flour and cornmeal mixture into the batter, give the whisk an extra turn or two to ensure the batter is well mixed. Adding cornmeal to a batter requires just a bit more mixing to develop the structure of the cake.

Simple Sparkle Flavorful and dense like cornbread, this cake makes a perfect brunch cake or light dessert topped with Sweetened Whipped Cream (page 6) and additional blueberries.

Individual Berry Trifles

12 servings | **PREP TIME: 25 Minutes** | **START TO FINISH: 3 Hours**

1   box white cake mix
    with pudding

1   cup water

¼   cup vegetable oil

3   egg whites

1   pint (2 cups)
    fresh blueberries

1   pint (2 cups)
    fresh raspberries

2   cups fresh strawberries,
    halved

⅓   cup granulated sugar

¼   cup raspberry-flavored
    liqueur or cranberry-
    raspberry juice

1   cup whipping cream

2   tablespoons
    powdered sugar

    Additional berries,
    if desired

1 Heat oven to 350°F. Make cake mix as directed, using water, oil and egg whites. Bake and cool as directed on box for 13 × 9-inch pan.

2 Meanwhile, in medium bowl, gently mix berries, granulated sugar and liqueur.

3 In chilled large bowl, beat whipping cream and powdered sugar with electric mixer on high speed until stiff peaks form.

4 Cut or tear cake into 1-inch pieces. In each of 12 glass dessert bowls, arrange half of the cake pieces. Spoon half of the berry mixture over cake; top with half of the whipped cream. Repeat layers. Cover; refrigerate at least 1 hour or up to 12 hours. Garnish with additional berries.

1 Serving: Calories 330; Total Fat 14g (Saturated Fat 6g, Trans Fat 0g); Cholesterol 20mg; Sodium 290mg; Total Carbohydrate 47g (Dietary Fiber 3g); Protein 3g **Exchanges:** 1 Starch, 2 Other Carbohydrate, 2½ Fat **Carbohydrate Choices:** 3

Sweet Secret Make one large trifle by layering the cake, berries and whipped cream in a 3-quart glass trifle bowl.

Sweet Secret Spread the fruit layers all the way to the edges of the trifle bowls so that the colors will be visible when the trifle is assembled.

Sweet Secret Using a chilled bowl and beaters ensures that the whipping cream will quickly form peaks when beaten.

Mixed-Berry Coffee Cake

8 servings | **PREP TIME: 15 Minutes** | **START TO FINISH: 1 Hour**

COFFEE CAKE

¾	cup granulated sugar
¼	cup butter, softened
1	egg
½	cup milk
1½	cups all-purpose flour
2	teaspoons baking powder
½	teaspoon salt
2	tablespoons granulated sugar
1	teaspoon ground cinnamon
1½	cups mixed fresh berries (such as blueberries, raspberries and blackberries)
⅓	cup sliced almonds

GLAZE

½	cup powdered sugar
¼	teaspoon vanilla
2 to 3	teaspoons milk

1 Heat oven to 350°F. Grease bottom and side of 9-inch round pan with shortening; lightly flour.

2 In large bowl, beat ¾ cup granulated sugar, the butter and egg with electric mixer on medium speed until fluffy. Beat in ½ cup milk just until blended. In separate small bowl, mix flour, baking powder and salt; stir into butter mixture. Spread batter in pan.

3 In medium bowl, stir together 2 tablespoons granulated sugar and the cinnamon. Add berries; toss until well coated. Spoon berry mixture over batter. Sprinkle with almonds.

4 Bake 35 to 45 minutes or until toothpick inserted in center comes out clean.

5 In small bowl, mix glaze ingredients until smooth and thin enough to drizzle. Drizzle over warm coffee cake. Serve warm.

1 Serving: Calories 310; Total Fat 9g (Saturated Fat 4.5g, Trans Fat 0g); Cholesterol 0mg; Sodium 330mg; Total Carbohydrate 53g (Dietary Fiber 2g); Protein 5g **Exchanges:** 1½ Starch, 2 Other Carbohydrate, 1½ Fat **Carbohydrate Choices:** 3½

Sweet Secret Try using sliced apples instead of the berries.

Berry Angel Delight

10 to 12 servings | **PREP TIME: 15 Minutes** | **START TO FINISH: 4 Hours 15 Minutes**

1 cup heavy whipping cream

2 tablespoons sugar

2 cups vanilla yogurt

1 round angel food cake
   (10 inch), cut into
   1-inch pieces

1 cup fresh blueberries

1 cup quartered
   fresh strawberries

1 cup fresh raspberries

1 In chilled medium bowl, beat whipping cream and sugar with electric mixer on high speed until stiff peaks form. Gently stir in yogurt.

2 Place cake pieces in large bowl; gently stir in yogurt mixture. In medium bowl, gently mix berries.

3 Spoon half of the cake mixture into 9-inch springform pan; press firmly in pan with rubber spatula. Top with half of the berries. Repeat with remaining cake mixture; press with spatula. Top with remaining berries. Cover and refrigerate at least 4 hours or overnight.

4 Run knife carefully along side of dessert to loosen; remove side of pan. Cut into wedges.

1 Serving: Calories 320; Total Fat 10g (Saturated Fat 6g, Trans Fat 0g); Cholesterol 35mg; Sodium 490mg; Total Carbohydrate 49g (Dietary Fiber 1g); Protein 7g **Exchanges:** 2½ Starch, ½ Fruit, ½ Other Carbohydrate, 1½ Fat **Carbohydrate Choices:** 3

Sweet Secret Any combination of fresh berries will work well in this refreshing dessert.

Simple Sparkle Just before serving, lightly dust fruit with powdered sugar sprinkled through a small strainer. Garnish with fresh fruit and mint.

Easy Berry Ice-Cream Cake

12 servings | **PREP TIME: 20 Minutes** | **START TO FINISH: 9 Hours 30 Minutes**

CAKE

2	cups Easy Scratch Cake Mix (page 7)
¼	cup butter, softened
¾	cup milk
1	teaspoon vanilla
2	eggs

FILLING

6	tablespoons fudge topping
3	cups fresh berries, such as blackberries, blueberries or raspberries
1½	quarts (6 cups) vanilla ice cream, slightly softened

1 Heat oven to 350°F. Grease 9-inch round pan with shortening; lightly flour.

2 In large bowl, beat cake ingredients with electric mixer on low speed 30 seconds, scraping bowl constantly. Beat on high speed 2 minutes, scraping bowl occasionally. Spread evenly in pan.

3 Bake 28 to 30 minutes or until toothpick inserted in center comes out clean. Cool 10 minutes. Remove from pan. Cool completely, about 30 minutes.

4 Wash and dry pan. Line with cooking parchment paper.

5 Using sharp knife, cut cake in half horizontally to make two layers. Set aside top layer. Place bottom of cake, cut side up, in pan. Spread with 3 tablespoons of the fudge topping; set aside.

6 In large bowl, carefully fold 2 cups of the berries into softened ice cream. Spread half of the ice cream evenly over cake in pan. Top with second cake layer rounded side down, pressing slightly into ice cream. Spread with remaining 3 tablespoons fudge topping; spread with remaining ice cream. Freeze about 8 hours or overnight or until ice cream is firm.

7 Just before serving, top with remaining 1 cup berries. Let stand 15 minutes before serving.

1 Serving: Calories 350; Total Fat 13g (Saturated Fat 8g, Trans Fat 0g); Cholesterol 70mg; Sodium 230mg; Total Carbohydrate 50g (Dietary Fiber 3g); Protein 6g **Exchanges:** 2 Starch, 0 Fruit, ½ Other Carbohydrate, 2½ Fat **Carbohydrate Choices:** 3

Sweet Secret Any of your favorite berries can be used for this ice-cream cake.

Sweet Secret To make lining the pan with parchment paper easier, crumple the paper before placing it in the pan.

Simple Sparkle Drizzle servings of this luscious dessert with additional fudge topping, or drizzle serving plates with fudge topping before placing ice-cream cake on them.

Strawberries and Cream Yogurt Cake

12 servings | **PREP TIME: 15 Minutes** | **START TO FINISH: 1 Hour 25 Minutes**

2 containers (6 oz each)
strawberry yogurt

1½ cups plus 2 teaspoons
granulated sugar

½ cup butter, melted

2 teaspoons vanilla

3 eggs

2¼ cups all-purpose flour

2 teaspoons baking powder

½ teaspoon salt

½ cup strawberry jam

1¼ cups quartered
fresh strawberries

Granulated or powdered
sugar, if desired

1 Heat oven to 350°F. Spray 13 × 9-inch pan with cooking spray.

2 In large bowl, stir together yogurt, 1½ cups of the granulated sugar, the melted butter and vanilla until well combined. Mix in eggs, 1 at a time, until well blended. Add flour, baking powder and salt. Beat with rubber spatula or wooden spoon until smooth.

3 Pour batter into pan, spreading evenly. Stir strawberry jam until smooth. Drop by teaspoonfuls on top of batter. Sprinkle with strawberries and remaining 2 teaspoons granulated sugar.

4 Bake 40 to 50 minutes or until toothpick inserted in center comes out clean. Cool 20 minutes. Sprinkle with granulated sugar.

1 Serving: Calories 260; Total Fat 9g (Saturated Fat 5g, Trans Fat 0g); Cholesterol 67mg; Sodium 191mg; Total Carbohydrate 41g (Dietary Fiber 0g); Protein 4g **Exchanges:** 1½ Starch, 2½ Other Carbohydrate, 2 Fat **Carbohydrate Choices:** 4

Sweet Secret Refrigerate this cake during humid weather or in humid climates. If stored at room temperature, this very moist cake may form mold.

Simple Sparkle To make this an extra-special dessert, serve it topped with whipped cream.

Raspberry-Vanilla Magic Custard Cake

8 servings | **PREP TIME: 20 Minutes** | **START TO FINISH: 3 Hours 10 Minutes**

1   cup fresh raspberries

4   eggs, separated

1   cup plus 2 teaspoons powdered sugar

½   cup butter, melted, cooled

1   teaspoon vanilla

1   cup all-purpose flour

2   cups whole milk

1 Heat oven to 325°F. Grease bottom and sides of 8- or 9-inch square pan with shortening or spray with cooking spray.

2 Arrange raspberries evenly in bottom of pan. In medium bowl, beat egg whites with electric mixer on high speed about 2 minutes or until stiff peaks form. Set aside.

3 In large bowl, beat egg yolks and 1 cup of the powdered sugar with electric mixer on medium speed about 5 minutes, scraping bowl occasionally, or until pale and smooth. Add butter and vanilla; beat until well blended. Add flour; beat just until flour is moistened (mixture will be very thick).

4 With mixer on low speed, gradually add milk; mix until smooth. Gently fold in egg whites. Mixture may appear slightly curdled. Pour evenly over raspberries.

5 Bake 45 to 50 minutes or just until center is set. Cool completely, about 2 hours. Cover and refrigerate until ready to serve but no longer than 24 hours. Just before serving, sprinkle with remaining 2 teaspoons powdered sugar. Cut cake into 4 squares; cut squares diagonally in half.

1 Serving: Calories 280; Total Fat 14g (Saturated Fat 8g, Trans Fat 0.5g); Cholesterol 35mg; Sodium 150mg; Total Carbohydrate 32g (Dietary Fiber 1g); Protein 5g **Exchanges:** 1½ Starch, ½ Other Carbohydrate, 2½ Fat **Carbohydrate Choices:** 2

Sweet Secret Be careful not to overbake this cake. It will continue to firm up while cooling.

Simple Sparkle For a special dessert, top with whipped cream and garnish with fresh raspberries.

Strawberry-Orange Dessert Shots

12 servings | **PREP TIME: 30 Minutes** | **START TO FINISH: 1 Hour**

1 container (6 oz) vanilla fat-free yogurt

2 oz cream cheese

¼ cup frozen (thawed) whipped topping

1 tablespoon orange-flavored liqueur

½ teaspoon grated orange peel

1 cup finely chopped fresh strawberries

48 cubes (¾ inch) angel food cake (2 cups)

6 teaspoons finely grated semisweet baking chocolate

1 In small bowl, mix yogurt, cream cheese, whipped topping, liqueur and orange peel until smooth and well blended. Spoon mixture into 1-quart resealable food-storage plastic bag; seal bag.

2 In each of 12 (2-oz) shot glasses, place 1 rounded teaspoon strawberries. Top each with 2 cake cubes. Cut corner from plastic bag and squeeze to pipe about 1 tablespoon yogurt mixture onto cake in each glass. Repeat layers. Sprinkle with grated chocolate.

3 Place shot glasses in 9-inch square pan. Refrigerate uncovered 30 minutes or until chilled but no longer than 3 hours.

1 Serving: Calories 60; Total Fat 2g (Saturated Fat 1g, Trans Fat 0g); Cholesterol 0mg; Sodium 80mg; Total Carbohydrate 9g (Dietary Fiber 0g); Protein 1g **Carbohydrate Choices:** ½

Strawberry-Pineapple Icebox Cake

8 servings | **PREP TIME: 20 Minutes** | **START TO FINISH: 12 Hours 20 Minutes**

38 cookies (from 10-oz package), thin-and-crispy golden or chocolate

1 can (8 oz) crushed pineapple, undrained

3 cups Sweetened Whipped Cream (page 6)

1½ cups chopped fresh strawberries

Fresh sliced strawberries, if desired

1 Line 9 x 5-inch loaf pan with foil, allowing foil to extend over edges.

2 Cut 8 of the cookies crosswise in half; set aside. Arrange 10 whole and 5 cookie halves in bottom of pan. Top with one-third of the pineapple. Spread about ¾ cup of the whipped cream evenly over pineapple. Arrange ½ cup strawberries over whipped cream. Repeat layers twice (use remaining cookie half for another use). Top with remaining whipped cream.

3 Cover with plastic wrap and refrigerate at least 12 hours or until cookies soften but no more than 30 hours.

4 To serve, use foil to lift cake from pan to serving platter; remove foil. Garnish with sliced strawberries. Serve immediately.

1 Serving: Calories 370; Total Fat 24g (Saturated Fat 12g, Trans Fat 0.5g); Cholesterol 60mg; Sodium 130mg; Total Carbohydrate 36g (Dietary Fiber 1g); Protein 2g **Exchanges:** 1 Starch, ½ Fruit, 1 Other Carbohydrate, 4½ Fat **Carbohydrate Choices:** 2½

Sweet Secret Use a sharp knife when cutting cookies or they may crumble slightly. Not to worry; just fit halves and any crumbs into the cookie layer.

Sweet Secret To test if the cake has been refrigerated long enough, insert a toothpick through the cookie layer. Cookies should be soft, and toothpick should glide easily through this layer.

Strawberry Angel Semifreddo

16 servings | **PREP TIME: 25 Minutes** | **START TO FINISH: 5 Hours 35 Minutes**

1 quart (1 lb) fresh strawberries, quartered (about 3 cups)

1 can (14 oz) sweetened condensed milk (not evaporated)

2 tablespoons orange-flavored liqueur or orange juice

1 teaspoon grated orange peel

1 loaf (8 oz) angel food cake

2 cups whipping cream

16 fresh strawberries, sliced

1 Line 2 (8 × 4-inch) loaf pans with plastic wrap, allowing 4 inches wrap to hang over short ends of pans. In food processor bowl with metal blade, place quartered strawberries. Cover; process with on-and-off pulses until almost pureed but with a few small pieces remaining. In large bowl, stir pureed strawberries, milk, liqueur and orange peel until well mixed.

2 Trim or brush any dark brown crust from angel food cake; cut cake into ¾-inch cubes. In large bowl, beat whipping cream with electric mixer on high speed until stiff peaks form. Fold whipped cream and cake cubes into strawberry mixture. Spoon mixture evenly into pans. Fold plastic wrap over mixture. Freeze at least 5 hours until firm.

3 Remove dessert from freezer 5 to 10 minutes before serving. Unwrap and unmold onto serving platter; remove plastic wrap. Garnish tops of loaves with strawberry slices.

1 Serving: Calories 230; Total Fat 12g (Saturated Fat 7g, Trans Fat 0g); Cholesterol 40mg; Sodium 150mg; Total Carbohydrate 27g (Dietary Fiber 1g); Protein 4g **Exchanges:** 1 Starch, 1 Fruit, 2 Fat **Carbohydrate Choices:** 2

Sweet Secret This is
a great make-ahead dessert. Store it wrapped tightly in the freezer up to 1 month. Use one pan for a small gathering, and keep the other for a future gathering. Or use both pans for a large gathering.

Sweet Secret
Semifreddo is Italian for "half cold." The term usually refers to a chilled or partially frozen dessert.

Angel Food Pudding Cake with Berries

24 servings | PREP TIME: 40 Minutes | START TO FINISH: 4 Hours 25 Minutes

CAKE

- 1 box angel food cake mix
- 1¼ cups water
- ¼ cup red, white and blue sprinkles

FILLING

- 4 containers (6 oz each) strawberry yogurt
- 1 container (12 oz) frozen whipped topping, thawed
- 1 box (4-serving size) vanilla instant pudding and pie filling mix
- 2 cups chopped fresh strawberries

TOPPING

- 1 cup fresh blueberries
- 1½ cups sliced fresh strawberries

1 Move oven rack to middle position. Heat oven to 350°F.

2 In large bowl, beat cake mix and water with electric mixer on low speed 30 seconds, then on medium speed 1 minute. Stir in sprinkles. Pour batter into ungreased 10-inch tube pan.

3 Bake 40 to 45 minutes or until deep golden brown. Cool completely upside down as directed on cake mix box, at least 1 hour. Run knife around sides of pan to loosen cake; turn cooled cake out onto cooling rack.

4 In large bowl, beat yogurt, 1½ cups of the whipped topping, and the pudding with whisk until well blended. Cut cake in half. Tear one of the halves into bite-size pieces. Place pieces in bottom of 13 × 9-inch pan. Sprinkle 1 cup of the chopped strawberries evenly over cake. Pour and spread half the yogurt filling on top. Tear other cake half into bite-size pieces. Repeat layers with remaining cake pieces, chopped strawberries and yogurt filling. Refrigerate at least 2 hours but no longer than 8 hours.

5 When ready to serve, spread remaining 3 cups whipped topping on top of cake. Decorate top of cake using blueberries to form large star in center. Arrange sliced strawberries around edges.

1 Serving: Calories 170; Total Fat 3.5g (Saturated Fat 3g, Trans Fat 0g); Cholesterol 0mg; Sodium 240mg; Total Carbohydrate 32g (Dietary Fiber 1g); Protein 3g **Exchanges:** 1 Starch, 1 Other Carbohydrate, ½ Fat **Carbohydrate Choices:** 2

Sweet Secret Short on time? Substitute purchased angel food cake, and add sprinkles on each layer of chopped strawberries.

Sweet Secret For a pretty look, use a glass baking dish to show off the layers.

Strawberry Shortcake Poke Bundt Cake

12 servings | PREP TIME: 35 Minutes | START TO FINISH: 4 Hours 15 Minutes

CAKE

- 1 box yellow cake mix with pudding
- 1 cup milk
- 4 oz cream cheese (from 8 oz package), softened
- 3 eggs

STRAWBERRY POKE MIXTURE

- 1½ cups sliced fresh strawberries
- ¼ cup granulated sugar
- 2 teaspoons lemon juice

CREAM CHEESE GLAZE

- ¾ cup powdered sugar
- 2 tablespoons butter, softened
- 1 oz cream cheese (from 8 oz package), softened
- 1 to 2 tablespoons milk
- ¼ teaspoon vanilla

GARNISH

- 1 cup sliced fresh strawberries

1 Heat oven to 325°F. Generously grease 10- or 12-cup fluted tube cake pan with shortening; lightly flour.

2 In large bowl, beat cake ingredients with electric mixer on low speed 1 minute, scraping bowl constantly. Increase speed to medium; beat 2 minutes. Pour into pan.

3 Bake 40 to 45 minutes or until toothpick inserted in center comes out clean. Cool 15 minutes.

4 Meanwhile, in food processor or blender, puree poke mixture ingredients until smooth. Transfer to 4-cup glass measuring cup; set aside. With handle of wooden spoon (¼ to ½ inch diameter), poke holes into cake every ½ inch, almost to bottom. Use wet paper towel to wipe end of spoon after each poke. Carefully pour poke mixture over holes in cake, using spoon to direct mixture into holes.

5 Cool 40 minutes; cover and refrigerate 2 hours. Run metal spatula around outer and inner sides of pan to loosen cake. Turn upside down onto serving platter.

6 In medium bowl, mix glaze ingredients with electric mixer on low speed until smooth. If too thick, add additional milk, 1 teaspoon at a time, until desired consistency. Glaze cake as desired; garnish with strawberries. Refrigerate any remaining cake.

1 Serving: Calories 280; Total Fat 9g (Saturated Fat 5g, Trans Fat 0g); Cholesterol 65mg; Sodium 340mg; Total Carbohydrate 46g (Dietary Fiber 1g); Protein 4g **Exchanges:** 1½ Starch, 1½ Other Carbohydrate, 1½ Fat **Carbohydrate Choices:** 3

Sweet Secret Slice and refrigerate strawberries ahead of time, and your cake will be ready to garnish when it's time to serve your guests.

Mango-Almond Coffee Cake

9 servings | **PREP TIME: 20 Minutes** | **START TO FINISH: 1 Hour 20 Minutes**

STREUSEL

- ⅓ cup all-purpose flour
- ⅓ cup packed dark brown sugar
- ⅓ cup old-fashioned oats
- ⅓ cup chopped slivered almonds
- 1 teaspoon ground cinnamon
- ¼ cup cold butter, cut into small pieces

CAKE

- 1 cup all-purpose flour
- ½ cup granulated sugar
- 1 teaspoon baking powder
- ½ teaspoon salt
- 1 teaspoon ground cinnamon
- ¼ cup cold butter, cut into small pieces
- ½ cup milk
- ½ teaspoon almond extract
- 1 egg, slightly beaten
- ¾ cup chopped (¼- to ½-inch pieces) ripe mango (from 1 medium)

1 Heat oven to 350°F. Grease bottom and sides of 8-inch square pan with shortening or spray with cooking spray. In small bowl, mix streusel ingredients with pastry blender or fork until crumbly; set aside.

2 In large bowl, combine 1 cup flour, the granulated sugar, baking powder, salt and 1 teaspoon cinnamon; mix well. Cut in ¼ cup butter using pastry blender or fork until mixture is crumbly. Stir in milk, almond extract and egg until dry ingredients are moistened.

3 Spread half of the batter (about ¾ cup) in pan, forming thin layer. Top with half of the mango; sprinkle with half of the streusel. Drizzle remaining batter evenly over streusel. Carefully spread remaining batter to completely cover streusel. Sprinkle with remaining mango and streusel.

4 Bake 40 to 45 minutes or until center is set when jiggled and toothpick inserted in moist spot near center comes out clean. Cool 15 minutes. Serve warm or cool.

1 Serving: Calories 300; Total Fat 13g (Saturated Fat 7g, Trans Fat 0g); Cholesterol 50mg; Sodium 290mg; Total Carbohydrate 39g (Dietary Fiber 2g); Protein 4g **Exchanges:** 1½ Starch, 1 Other Carbohydrate, 2½ Fat **Carbohydrate Choices:** 2½

Sweet Secret Frozen mangoes (do not thaw) or refrigerated mango slices in light syrup can be substituted for the fresh ones. Drain refrigerated mangoes and pat dry with a paper towel. Be sure to chop any mango used into the size indicated in the recipe to avoid wet spots in the cake.

Mango-Mojito Mug Cake

2 mug cakes | PREP TIME: 10 Minutes | START TO FINISH: 20 Minutes

1 cup chopped mango

1½ teaspoons fresh lime juice

1½ teaspoons rum extract

1 teaspoon chopped fresh mint

2 tablespoons butter, melted

1 egg

¾ cup Easy Scratch Cake Mix (page 7)

Whipped topping or pressurized whipped cream, if desired

1 In small food processor or blender container, combine mango, lime juice, rum extract and mint. Cover and process about 1 minute or until smooth. Reserve 1 tablespoon mango mixture; set aside.

2 In small bowl, beat butter, egg and remaining mango mixture with whisk. Stir in cake mix until blended.

3 Divide batter between two 10-oz or larger microwavable mugs. Microwave uncovered on High 2½ to 3½ minutes or until toothpick inserted in center comes out clean and cake pulls away from sides of mugs. Cool 5 minutes.

4 Top with whipped topping. Drizzle with reserved mango mixture.

1 Mug Cake: Calories 440; Total Fat 15g (Saturated Fat 8g, Trans Fat 0g); Cholesterol 125mg; Sodium 350mg; Total Carbohydrate 66g (Dietary Fiber 2g); Protein 7g **Exchanges:** 1 Starch, 1 Fruit, 2½ Other Carbohydrate, ½ Medium-Fat Meat, 2½ Fat **Carbohydrate Choices:** 4½

Sweet Secret If fresh mango isn't available, use refrigerated mango, drained, instead of the fresh.

Simple Sparkle Add one or two fresh mint leaves on top of the whipped topping.

Rhubarb Coffee Cake

15 servings | **PREP TIME: 20 Minutes** | **START TO FINISH: 1 Hour 35 Minutes**

1 box yellow cake mix with pudding

¾ cup milk

1 teaspoon vanilla

3 eggs

1 package (3 oz) cream cheese, softened

2 cups chopped fresh rhubarb

½ cup all-purpose flour

¾ cup sugar

¼ cup butter, softened

1 Heat oven to 325°F. Spray bottom and sides of 13 x 9-inch pan with baking spray with flour.

2 In large bowl, beat cake mix, milk, vanilla, eggs and cream cheese with electric mixer on low speed 1 minute, then on medium speed 2 minutes, scraping bowl frequently. Set aside.

3 In medium bowl, toss rhubarb and ¼ cup of the flour. Fold rhubarb into batter; spread in pan. In small bowl, mix remaining ¼ cup flour, the sugar and butter until coarse crumbs form. Sprinkle over batter.

4 Bake 35 to 42 minutes or until lightly browned and toothpick inserted in center comes out clean. Cool about 30 minutes to serve warm, or cool completely.

1 Serving: Calories 240; Total Fat 7g (Saturated Fat 4g, Trans Fat 0g); Cholesterol 60mg; Sodium 260mg; Total Carbohydrate 39g (Dietary Fiber 0g); Protein 3g **Exchanges:** 1 Starch, 1½ Other Carbohydrate, 1½ Fat **Carbohydrate Choices:** 2½

Sweet Secret If you use frozen rhubarb, measure it while it's still frozen; then partially thaw and chop. Thaw rhubarb completely in a colander and drain, but do not press out the liquid.

Sweet Secret Use a serrated knife to easily cut the cake, and dip it in hot water before cutting each piece.

Raspberry-Rhubarb Coffee Cake

9 servings | PREP TIME: **25 Minutes** | START TO FINISH: **2 Hours**

FILLING

- 3 cups chopped fresh or frozen rhubarb
- ¼ cup sugar
- 3 tablespoons water
- 1 tablespoon cornstarch
- 1 cup fresh raspberries

CAKE

- ⅓ cup butter, softened
- ½ teaspoon vanilla
- 2 eggs
- 1½ cups Easy Scratch Cake Mix (page 7)
- ½ cup sour cream

TOPPING

- ¼ cup packed brown sugar
- ½ cup chopped pecans
- ½ cup old-fashioned oats
- 2 tablespoons all-purpose flour
- ¼ teaspoon ground cinnamon
- ¼ cup cold butter

1 Heat oven to 350°F. Grease 8- or 9-inch square pan with shortening or spray with cooking spray.

2 In 2-quart saucepan, cook rhubarb, sugar, water and cornstarch over medium-low heat 8 to 10 minutes, stirring constantly, or until thickened. Cool 5 minutes. Carefully fold in raspberries. Set aside.

3 In medium bowl, beat ⅓ cup butter, the vanilla and eggs with electric mixer on medium speed about 1 minute, scraping bowl occasionally, until well blended. Add cake mix and sour cream. Beat until well blended (batter will be thick). Spoon half of the batter evenly into pan. Carefully spoon rhubarb mixture over batter. Spoon remaining batter evenly over rhubarb mixture.

4 In small bowl, mix brown sugar, pecans, oats, flour and cinnamon until well blended. Cut in butter with pastry blender or 2 forks until crumbly. Sprinkle over cake batter.

5 Bake 55 to 60 minutes or until toothpick inserted in center comes out clean. Cool 30 minutes.

1 Serving: Calories 390; Total Fat 21g (Saturated Fat 10g, Trans Fat 0.5g); Cholesterol 80mg; Sodium 220mg; Total Carbohydrate 45g (Dietary Fiber 3g); Protein 5g **Exchanges:** 1 Starch, ½ Fruit, 1½ Other Carbohydrate, ½ Medium-Fat Meat, 3½ Fat **Carbohydrate Choices:** 3

Sweet Secret Serve this coffee cake warm, topped with additional raspberries, for the best flavor and texture. Enjoy it with a cup of coffee!

Simple Sparkle There's no reason this delicious coffee cake wouldn't make a fabulous dessert, too! Simply top servings of it with a dollop of whipped cream.

Tropical Trifle

10 servings | **PREP TIME: 35 Minutes** | **START TO FINISH: 4 Hours 40 Minutes**

2 cups milk

1 box (4-serving size) vanilla instant pudding and pie filling mix

1 teaspoon grated orange peel

1 round angel food cake (12 to 15 oz), cut into 1-inch cubes

2 tablespoons orange-flavored liqueur or orange juice

1 can (20 oz) pineapple tidbits, well drained

2 kiwifruit, peeled, cut into ¼-inch slices

1 ripe mango, seed removed, peeled and cut into cubes

2 cups fresh strawberries, cut in half

¼ cup shredded or flaked coconut, toasted (see tip)

1 In medium bowl, beat milk and pudding mix with whisk 2 minutes. Stir in orange peel. Let stand 5 minutes.

2 In 3½-quart trifle bowl, place half of cake cubes. Drizzle with 1 tablespoon of the liqueur. Spoon 1 cup of the pudding over cake. Layer with pineapple, kiwifruit and remaining cake cubes. Drizzle with remaining 1 tablespoon liqueur. Spoon remaining pudding over cake. Layer with mango and strawberries. Cover; refrigerate at least 4 hours but no longer than 8 hours.

3 Just before serving, sprinkle trifle with toasted coconut. Spoon down to bottom of dish to scoop out servings.

1 Serving: Calories 240; Total Fat 2.5g (Saturated Fat 1.5g, Trans Fat 0g); Cholesterol 0mg; Sodium 430mg; Total Carbohydrate 48g (Dietary Fiber 2g); Protein 5g **Carbohydrate Choices:** 3

Sweet Secret To remove the peel and seed from mango, use a sharp knife to make a cut through one side of mango, sliding knife next to seed. Repeat on other side of seed, making two large pieces. Make cuts in crosshatch fashion through flesh just to peel; bend peel back and carefully slide knife between peel and flesh to separate. Discard peel; cut flesh into cubes.

Sweet Secret To toast coconut, sprinkle in ungreased heavy skillet. Cook over medium heat 5 to 7 minutes, stirring frequently until coconut begins to brown, then stirring constantly until coconut is light brown.

Sweet Secret For Banana-Raspberry-Orange Trifle, substitute sliced bananas (sprinkled with lemon juice), fresh raspberries and canned mandarin orange segments for the pineapple, mango and strawberries. Experiment to come up with your favorite combination!

pumpkin, carrot & zucchini cakes

Pumpkin-Layered Magic Cake

18 servings | **PREP TIME: 25 Minutes** | **START TO FINISH: 5 Hours 50 Minutes**

1 box yellow cake mix with pudding

1 cup water

½ cup vegetable oil

3 eggs

1 can (15 oz) pumpkin (not pumpkin pie mix)

1 cup packed brown sugar

1 cup half-and-half

3 eggs

2 teaspoons pumpkin pie spice

½ teaspoon salt

TOPPING

1 package (8 oz) cream cheese, softened

¾ cup powdered sugar

1 teaspoon vanilla

⅛ teaspoon salt

2 cups heavy whipping cream

Pumpkin pie spice

1 Heat oven to 350°F. Grease bottom only of 13 × 9-inch pan with shortening or cooking spray.

2 In large bowl, beat cake mix, water, oil and 3 eggs with electric mixer on low speed until moistened. Scrape bowl; beat 2 minutes on medium speed. Spread in pan.

3 In another large bowl, mix pumpkin, brown sugar, half-and-half, 3 eggs, pumpkin pie spice and ½ teaspoon salt with whisk until smooth. Carefully spoon pumpkin mixture over batter in pan.

4 Bake 48 to 53 minutes or until cake is set when touched lightly in center. Cool 30 minutes. Refrigerate at least 4 hours or until chilled.

5 In large bowl, with electric mixer on low speed, beat cream cheese, powdered sugar, vanilla and ⅛ teaspoon salt until smooth. Gradually increase speed to high, add whipping cream, and beat until stiff peaks form. Spread over chilled cake. Sprinkle lightly with pumpkin pie spice. Store covered in refrigerator.

1 Serving: Calories 400; Total Fat 24g (Saturated Fat 12g, Trans Fat 0.5g); Cholesterol 115mg; Sodium 340mg; Total Carbohydrate 41g (Dietary Fiber 1g); Protein 4g **Exchanges:** 1½ Starch, 1 Other Carbohydrate, 4½ Fat **Carbohydrate Choices:** 3

Sweet Secret Short on time? Bake the cake the day before serving and top it the next day. Or prepare the entire cake the day before serving.

Sweet Secret Change it up and sprinkle the top of the cake with chopped pecans, chopped candy bars or crumbled soft ginger cookies.

Pumpkin-Spiced Creamy Rum Poke Cake

15 servings | **PREP TIME: 25 Minutes** | **START TO FINISH: 4 Hours 10 Minutes**

FILLING

- 1 package (8 oz) cream cheese, softened
- 1 can (14 oz) sweetened condensed milk (not evaporated)
- ¼ cup Caribbean spiced rum cream liqueur

CAKE

- 1½ cups sugar
- 1 cup vegetable oil
- 4 eggs
- 1 can (15 oz) pumpkin (not pumpkin pie mix)
- 2¾ cups all-purpose flour
- 2 teaspoons baking powder
- 2 teaspoons pumpkin pie spice
- 1 teaspoon salt
- ½ teaspoon baking soda

TOPPING

- 1½ cups whipping cream
- 3 tablespoons Caribbean spiced rum cream liqueur
- 1 tablespoon sugar

1 Heat oven to 350°F. Grease bottom only of 13 × 9-inch pan with shortening or spray with cooking spray.

2 In medium bowl, beat cream cheese with electric mixer on medium speed 1 to 2 minutes or until smooth. Add sweetened condensed milk and ¼ cup liqueur; beat, scraping bowl frequently, until smooth. Cover and refrigerate while preparing cake.

3 In large bowl, beat 1½ cups sugar, the oil, eggs and pumpkin with electric mixer on low speed 1 minute, scraping bowl constantly. Add flour, baking powder, pumpkin pie spice, salt and baking soda. Beat on medium speed 2 minutes. Pour evenly into pan.

4 Bake 30 to 35 minutes or until toothpick inserted in center comes out clean. Cool 10 minutes.

5 With handle of wooden spoon (¼ to ½ inch diameter), poke holes halfway down into cake every inch, wiping spoon handle occasionally to prevent sticking. Cool completely on cooling rack, about 1 hour.

6 Pour cream cheese mixture over cake, working back and forth to fill holes. (Some filling should remain on top of cake.) Cool completely, about 1 hour.

7 In chilled medium bowl, beat whipping cream, 3 tablespoons liqueur and 1 tablespoon sugar with electric mixer on low speed until thickened. Gradually increase speed to high and beat just until stiff peaks form. Carefully spread over cake. Cover loosely; refrigerate about 1 hour or until chilled but no longer than 48 hours. Sprinkle with additional pumpkin pie spice, if desired.

1 Serving: Calories 560; Total Fat 32g (Saturated Fat 12g, Trans Fat 0.5g); Cholesterol 105mg; Sodium 390mg; Total Carbohydrate 58g (Dietary Fiber 1g); Protein 8g **Carbohydrate Choices:** 4

Sweet Secret Serve this decadent dessert with cups of coffee spiked with more of the spiced rum-delicious!

Pumpkin Praline Cake

15 servings | PREP TIME: 15 Minutes | START TO FINISH: 2 Hours 30 Minutes

1 cup packed brown sugar
½ cup butter
¼ cup heavy whipping cream
¾ cup chopped pecans
2¾ cups all-purpose flour
2 teaspoons baking powder
2 teaspoons ground cinnamon
1 teaspoon salt
½ teaspoon baking soda
½ teaspoon ground nutmeg
¼ teaspoon ground cloves
1½ cups granulated sugar
1 cup vegetable oil
4 eggs
1 can (15 oz) pumpkin (not pumpkin pie mix)

1 Heat oven to 350ºF. In 2-quart saucepan, heat brown sugar, butter and whipping cream over medium heat, stirring occasionally, until butter is melted. Pour into ungreased 13 x 9-inch pan. Sprinkle with pecans.

2 In small bowl, mix flour, baking powder, cinnamon, salt, baking soda, nutmeg and cloves; set aside. In large bowl, beat granulated sugar, oil, eggs and pumpkin with electric mixer on medium speed 1 minute, scraping bowl constantly. Gradually beat in flour mixture 2 minutes, scraping bowl occasionally. Carefully spoon batter over pecan mixture.

3 Bake 30 to 35 minutes or until toothpick inserted in center comes out clean. Cool 10 minutes. Place heatproof serving tray upside down over pan; turn tray and pan over. Leave pan over cake a few minutes. Cool completely, about 1 hour 30 minutes.

1 Serving: Calories 495; Total Fat 28g (Saturated Fat 8g, Trans Fat 0g); Cholesterol 75mg; Sodium 330mg; Total Carbohydrate 56g (Dietary Fiber 2g); Protein 5g **Exchanges:** 2 Starch, 2 Fruit, 5 Fat **Carbohydrate Choices:** 4

Simple Sparkle Crown servings of this autumn cake with whipped cream and whole pecans.

Simple Sparkle Sprinkle ground cinnamon over dessert plates for a restaurant-fancy finish.

Slow-Cooker Pumpkin Cake with Cream Cheese Frosting

16 servings | **PREP TIME: 15 Minutes** | **START TO FINISH: 4 Hours 25 Minutes**

CAKE

1	box yellow cake mix with pudding
1	cup canned pumpkin (not pumpkin pie mix)
½	cup water
⅓	cup vegetable oil
4	eggs
1½	teaspoons pumpkin pie spice

FROSTING

4	oz cream cheese, softened
⅓	cup butter, softened
1	teaspoon vanilla
2	cups powdered sugar

GARNISH

½	cup chopped pecans or walnuts, if desired

1 Line bottom and sides of 5½- or 6-quart slow cooker with 1 piece of cooking parchment paper; trim edges if needed. Spray with cooking spray.

2 In large bowl, beat cake mix, pumpkin, water, vegetable oil, eggs and pumpkin pie spice with electric mixer on low speed 1 minute, scraping bowl constantly. Increase speed to medium; beat 2 minutes. Pour batter into slow cooker.

3 Place folded, clean dish towel under cover of cooker. Cook on High setting 1 hour 45 minutes to 2 hours, carefully rotating slow cooker's ceramic insert 180 degrees (leaving cover on) after every 45 minutes or until toothpick inserted in center comes out clean. Uncover and transfer ceramic insert to cooling rack. Let stand 10 minutes.

4 Using parchment paper, carefully lift cake out of ceramic insert and transfer to cooling rack. Cool completely, about 2 hours. Remove parchment paper.

5 Meanwhile, in medium bowl, beat cream cheese, butter and vanilla with electric mixer on low speed until smooth. Gradually beat in powdered sugar, 1 cup at a time, until smooth and spreadable. Spread over cake. Sprinkle with pecans.

1 Serving: Calories 290; Total Fat 13g (Saturated Fat 6g, Trans Fat 0g); Cholesterol 65mg; Sodium 270mg; Total Carbohydrate 39g (Dietary Fiber 0g); Protein 3g **Exchanges:** 1 Starch, 1½ Other Carbohydrate, 2½ Fat **Carbohydrate Choices:** 2½

Easy Pumpkin Pie Cake

16 servings | **PREP TIME: 10 Minutes** | **START TO FINISH: 1 Hour 25 Minutes**

2 eggs

½ cup sugar

1 teaspoon ground cinnamon

½ teaspoon salt

½ teaspoon ground ginger

⅛ teaspoon ground cloves

1 can (15 oz) pumpkin (not pumpkin pie mix)

1 can (12 oz) evaporated milk

1 box yellow cake mix with pudding

½ cup butter, melted

¾ cup chopped pecans

Sweetened Whipped Cream (page 6), if desired

1 Heat oven to 350°F. Grease 13 × 9-inch pan with shortening or cooking spray.

2 In large bowl, beat eggs, sugar, cinnamon, salt, ginger, cloves, pumpkin and evaporated milk with whisk until well combined. Pour into pan.

3 In medium bowl, mix cake mix and melted butter until well combined (mixture will be lumpy). Stir in chopped pecans. Sprinkle mixture evenly over pumpkin mixture in pan.

4 Bake 40 to 45 minutes or until center is set and edges are golden brown. Cool 30 minutes before serving.

1 Serving: Calories 260; Total Fat 12g (Saturated Fat 5g, Trans Fat 0g); Cholesterol 40mg; Sodium 350mg; Total Carbohydrate 34g (Dietary Fiber 1g); Protein 3g **Exchanges:** ½ Starch, 2 Other Carbohydrate, 2½ Fat **Carbohydrate Choices:** 2

Sweet Secret
If you like, you can make the cake up to 3 days ahead and then refrigerate until cold. Top with whipped cream just before serving.

Simple Sparkle
Stir a little cinnamon into your whipped cream for an extra-festive touch.

Pumpkin Bundt Cake with Cream Cheese Glaze

12 servings | **PREP TIME: 15 Minutes** | **START TO FINISH: 2 Hours 10 Minutes**

CAKE

- 1 box yellow cake mix with pudding
- 1 cup canned pumpkin (not pumpkin pie mix)
- ½ cup water
- ⅓ cup vegetable oil
- 1 tablespoon pumpkin pie spice
- 4 eggs

GLAZE

- ⅓ cup cream cheese creamy ready-to-spread frosting (from 16-oz container)

1 Heat oven to 325°F. Grease 12-cup fluted tube cake pan with shortening; lightly flour.

2 In large bowl, beat cake mix, pumpkin, water, oil, pumpkin pie spice and eggs with electric mixer on low speed until moistened, then on medium speed 2 minutes, scraping bowl occasionally. Pour batter into pan.

3 Bake 40 to 45 minutes or until toothpick inserted in center comes out clean. Cool 10 minutes; remove from pan to cooling rack. Cool completely, about 1 hour.

4 In small microwavable bowl, microwave frosting uncovered on Low (10%) 10 to 20 seconds, stirring until thick drizzling consistency. Spoon over cake.

1 Serving: Calories 250; Total Fat 10g (Saturated Fat 3g, Trans Fat 0g); Cholesterol 60mg; Sodium 300mg; Total Carbohydrate 37g (Dietary Fiber 1g); Protein 3g **Exchanges:** 1 Starch, 1½ Other Carbohydrate, 2 Fat **Carbohydrate Choices:** 2½

Sweet Secret You can make this cake a day ahead, and frost it just before serving.

Simple Sparkle Sprinkle the cake with powdered sugar instead of drizzling with the frosting. Or top servings with whipped cream.

Pumpkin Truffle Pound Cake

16 servings | **PREP TIME: 25 Minutes** | **START TO FINISH: 2 Hours 45 Minutes**

CAKE

- ⅔ cup (from 14-oz can) sweetened condensed milk (not evaporated)
- 1 cup semisweet chocolate chips (6 oz)
- 3 cups all-purpose flour
- 2 teaspoons baking powder
- 1 teaspoon baking soda
- 4 teaspoons pumpkin pie spice
- ¼ teaspoon salt
- 1½ cups butter, softened
- 1 cup granulated sugar
- ½ cup packed brown sugar
- 6 eggs
- 1 cup canned pumpkin (not pumpkin pie mix)

ICING

- ¼ cup butter
- 1 cup powdered sugar
- 1 teaspoon vanilla
- 1 to 2 tablespoons milk

1. Heat oven to 350°F. Grease 12-cup fluted tube cake pan with shortening; lightly flour.

2. In 1-quart saucepan, heat condensed milk and chocolate chips over medium-low heat, stirring occasionally, until chocolate is melted. Remove from heat; set aside.

3. In medium bowl, mix flour, baking powder, baking soda, pumpkin pie spice and salt until blended; set aside.

4. In large bowl, beat 1½ cups butter, the granulated sugar and brown sugar with electric mixer on medium speed about 2 minutes or until well blended. Add eggs, one at a time, beating well after each addition. On low speed, beat in flour mixture in three additions alternately with pumpkin until well blended (batter will be thick).

5. Spoon two-thirds of the batter (about 5 cups) into pan. Using the back of the spoon, push some batter up against the inner and outer sides of the pan to make a 1-inch-high edging all around. Stir chocolate mixture; spoon into center of batter, being careful not to touch sides of pan. Spoon remaining cake batter (about 2 cups) over filling; smooth top.

6. Bake 55 to 65 minutes or until toothpick inserted in center comes out clean and center of crack is dry to touch. Cool 15 minutes. Place cooling rack upside down over pan; turn rack and pan over; remove pan. Cool completely, about 1 hour.

7. Place cake on serving plate. In 1-quart saucepan, heat ¼ cup butter over medium heat, stirring occasionally, until golden brown. Pour browned butter into medium bowl; stir in powdered sugar, vanilla and milk, 1 tablespoon at a time, until spreadable (mixture will thicken). Let stand 1 to 2 minutes or until slightly cool; stir. Drizzle over cake.

1 Serving: Calories 510; Total Fat 27g (Saturated Fat 16g, Trans Fat 1g); Cholesterol 135mg; Sodium 360mg; Total Carbohydrate 60g (Dietary Fiber 2g); Protein 6g **Exchanges:** 2 Starch, 2 Other Carbohydrate, 5 Fat **Carbohydrate Choices:** 4

Sweet Secret Be sure to use canned pumpkin, not pumpkin pie mix, for this yummy, incredible pound cake. Pumpkin pie mix contains sugar and spices-not just pumpkin.

Secrets to Great Slow-Cooker Cakes

Bake cakes in your slow cooker? Yes! Free up your oven for other dishes for a meal, keep your kitchen cool on hot days or simply for the fun of it. Here are great tips on how to do it successfully.

- **Line Your Slow Cooker** Use a piece of parchment paper to line the bottom and sides of your slow cooker. Make it easier to work with by crumpling it loosely before placing the paper in the slow cooker.

- **Spray Parchment Paper with Cooking Spray** It's necessary to spray the parchment paper with cooking spray to help the cake release easily after cooking.

- **Use a Folded Towel Under the Cover** As the cake cooks, condensation builds up on the inside of the cover, causing moisture to drip down on the cake, making it difficult for the cake to cook through. The folded towel will absorb the moisture the cake creates, eliminating this problem.

- **Rotate Insert 180 Degrees** Many slow cookers have hot spots, where one side of the heating element can cause cakes to burn on that side. To alleviate the problem, rotate the slow cooker insert (with the cover left on) 180 degrees as directed in the recipe.

- **Leave the Cover On** Each time you lift the lid of a slow cooker, the amount of heat that escapes will cost you about 30 minutes of cooking time. So don't peek until the cake has cooked for the minimum time given in the recipe. Cover and bake longer if necessary, until the doneness has been reached.

- **Cool Cake in Insert** The cake is cooled in the insert, usually uncovered. Cool it on a cooling rack so air can get to all sides. Remove the cake from the insert after 10 minutes to finish cooling. Use the parchment paper to lift the cake from the slow cooker.

- **Cool As Directed** Cakes need time to cool so they won't be gummy. Refer to the specific directions in each recipe for the proper cooling time.

- **Deal with Dark Spots** Each slow cooker is different. Dark spots and/or hard edges may happen when using a slow cooker to bake a cake from the insert. If your cake develops these, you can either leave them as is, cover the areas with frosting or cut them off before frosting or serving.

Pumpkin-Chocolate Swirl Cake with Chocolate Ganache

12 servings | **PREP TIME: 20 Minutes** | **START TO FINISH: 2 Hours 25 Minutes**

CAKE

- 1 box spice cake mix with pudding
- 1 cup canned pumpkin (not pumpkin pie mix)
- ½ cup water
- ⅓ cup vegetable oil
- 4 eggs
- ½ teaspoon pumpkin pie spice
- ⅓ cup chopped semisweet baking chocolate
- 2 tablespoons unsweetened baking cocoa

CHOCOLATE GANACHE

- ¼ cup heavy whipping cream
- ½ cup chopped semisweet baking chocolate

1 Heat oven to 325°F. Grease 10- or 12-cup fluted tube cake pan with shortening; lightly flour.

2 In large bowl, beat cake mix, pumpkin, water, vegetable oil, eggs and pumpkin pie spice with electric mixer on low speed 1 minute, scraping bowl constantly. Increase speed to medium; beat 2 minutes.

3 Pour 1 cup of the batter into the glass measuring cup you used for measuring the water and oil. Stir in ⅓ cup semisweet chocolate and the baking cocoa until well combined. Pour half of the pumpkin batter into pan. Spoon chocolate batter over batter in pan. Top with remaining pumpkin batter.

4 Bake 40 to 45 minutes or until toothpick inserted in center comes out clean. Cool 15 minutes. Turn upside down onto cooling rack or heatproof serving plate; remove pan. Cool completely, about 1 hour. Place cake on serving plate.

5 In microwavable bowl, microwave cream uncovered on High 45 to 60 seconds or until cream just begins to simmer. Add ½ cup semisweet chocolate, and stir until smooth. Cool 5 minutes. Drizzle over cake.

1 Serving: Calories 190; Total Fat 15g (Saturated Fat 6g, Trans Fat 0g); Cholesterol 70mg; Sodium 55mg; Total Carbohydrate 10g (Dietary Fiber 2g); Protein 3g **Exchanges:** ½ Starch, 3 Fat **Carbohydrate Choices:** ½

Sweet Secret If desired, you can swap the spice cake mix for yellow cake mix, and bump up the pumpkin pie spice to 1½ teaspoons.

Sweet Secret This cake was photographed using a specialty fluted tube cake pan. Deeper pans may require an additional 2 to 7 minutes of bake time.

Spiced Pumpkin–Chocolate Chip Mug Cake

1 mug cake | **PREP TIME: 10 Minutes** | **START TO FINISH: 20 Minutes**

CAKE

- **2** tablespoons butter
- **¼** cup canned pumpkin (not pumpkin pie mix)
- **2** tablespoons milk
- **½** teaspoon vanilla
- **½** cup Easy Scratch Cake Mix (page 7)
- **¼** teaspoon pumpkin pie spice
- **1** tablespoon miniature semisweet chocolate chips

TOPPING

- **¼** cup heavy whipping cream
- **1** teaspoon powdered sugar
- **⅛** teaspoon pumpkin pie spice
- **1** tablespoon caramel topping
- **1** teaspoon miniature semisweet chocolate chips

1 In 12-oz microwavable coffee mug, microwave butter on High 30 to 45 seconds or until melted. Stir in pumpkin, milk, vanilla, cake mix and ¼ teaspoon pumpkin spice with fork until well blended. Stir in 1 tablespoon chocolate chips.

2 Microwave uncovered on High 1 to 2 minutes or until toothpick inserted in center comes out clean and cake pulls from sides of mug. Cool 5 minutes.

3 Meanwhile, in small bowl, beat whipping cream with electric mixer on medium speed until soft peaks form. Add powdered sugar and ⅛ teaspoon pumpkin pie spice; beat on medium speed until stiff peaks form. Spoon whipped topping onto cake. Drizzle with caramel topping. Sprinkle with 1 teaspoon chocolate chips.

1 Mug Cake: Calories 1180; Total Fat 48g (Saturated Fat 29g, Trans Fat 1.5g); Cholesterol 130mg; Sodium 900mg; Total Carbohydrate 174g (Dietary Fiber 5g); Protein 12g **Exchanges:** 4 Starch, 7½ Other Carbohydrate, 9 Fat **Carbohydrate Choices:** 11½

Sweet Secret Make sure that the mug holds at least 12 ounces of liquid or cake may overflow.

Sweet Secret This indulgent dessert is perfect for sharing. Grab an extra spoon and enjoy it together!

Sweet Secret Fresh whipped cream is divine, but you could skip whipping the cream and use a little whipped cream from an aerosol can instead. Sprinkle with the pumpkin pie spice and drizzle with the caramel topping.

Carrot Cake

12 to 16 servings | **PREP TIME: 20 Minutes** | **START TO FINISH: 1 Hour 5 Minutes**

CAKE

- 1½ cups granulated sugar
- 1 cup vegetable oil
- 3 eggs
- 2 cups all-purpose flour
- 2 teaspoons ground cinnamon
- 1 teaspoon baking soda
- 1 teaspoon vanilla
- ½ teaspoon salt
- 3 cups shredded carrots (5 medium)
- 1 cup coarsely chopped walnuts

FROSTING

- 1 package (8 oz) cream cheese, softened
- ¼ cup butter, softened
- 2 to 3 teaspoons milk
- 1 teaspoon vanilla
- 4 cups powdered sugar
- Ground nutmeg, if desired

1 Heat oven to 350°F. Grease bottom and sides of one 13 × 9-inch pan with shortening; lightly flour.

2 In large bowl, beat granulated sugar, oil and eggs with electric mixer on low speed about 30 seconds or until blended. Add flour, cinnamon, baking soda, 1 teaspoon vanilla and the salt; beat on low speed 1 minute. Stir in carrots and walnuts. Pour into pan(s).

3 Bake 40 to 45 minutes, or until toothpick inserted in center comes out clean. Cool in pan on cooling rack completely, about 1 hour.

4 In medium bowl, beat cream cheese, butter, milk and vanilla with electric mixer on low speed until smooth. Gradually beat in powdered sugar, 1 cup at a time, until smooth and spreadable. Frost cake with frosting. Sprinkle nutmeg over frosting. Store in refrigerator.

1 Serving: Calories 440; Total Fat 26g (Saturated Fat 3.5g, Trans Fat 0g); Cholesterol 55mg; Sodium 230mg; Total Carbohydrate 46g (Dietary Fiber 2g); Protein 6g **Exchanges:** 2 Starch, 1 Other Carbohydrate, 5 Fat **Carbohydrate Choices:** 3

Sweet Secret Go nuts! Use pecans, almonds or hazelnuts instead of walnuts.

Sweet Secret Save yourself time by using a 16-ounce container of cream cheese creamy ready-to-spread frosting instead of the from-scratch recipe.

Gluten-Free Carrot Cake

12 servings | **PREP TIME: 15 Minutes** | **START TO FINISH: 1 Hour 55 Minutes**

CAKE

- 1 box gluten-free yellow cake mix
- ⅔ cup water
- ½ cup butter, softened
- ½ teaspoon ground cinnamon
- ¼ teaspoon ground nutmeg
- 2 teaspoons gluten-free vanilla
- 3 eggs
- 1 cup finely shredded carrots (2 medium)
- ¼ cup finely chopped pecans or walnuts

FROSTING

- 4 oz (half of 8-oz package) cream cheese, softened
- 2 tablespoons butter
- ½ teaspoon gluten-free vanilla
- 1 to 3 teaspoons milk
- 2 cups powdered sugar
- ¼ cup coconut toasted, if desired

1 Heat oven to 350°F. Grease bottom only of 8- or 9-inch square pan with shortening or cooking spray (without flour).

2 In a large bowl, beat cake mix, water, ½ cup butter, the cinnamon, nutmeg, 2 teaspoons vanilla and the eggs on low speed 30 seconds. Beat on medium speed 2 minutes, scraping bowl occasionally. With spoon, stir in carrots and pecans. Spread in pan.

3 Bake 8-inch pan 36 to 41 minutes, 9-inch pan 33 to 38 minutes, or until toothpick comes out clean. Cool completely, about 1 hour.

4 In a medium bowl, beat cream cheese, 2 tablespoons butter, ½ teaspoon vanilla and 1 teaspoon milk until smooth. Gradually beat in powdered sugar, 1 cup at a time, until smooth and spreadable. If frosting is too thick, beat in more milk, a few drops at a time. Spread frosting over cake. Sprinkle with coconut.

1 Serving: Calories 420; Total Fat 16g (Saturated Fat 9g, Trans Fat 0g); Cholesterol 90mg; Sodium 310mg; Total Carbohydrate 66g (Dietary Fiber 0g); Protein 3g **Exchanges:** 1 Starch, 3½ Other Carbohydrate, 3 Fat **Carbohydrate Choices:** 4½

Cooking Gluten Free? Always read labels to make sure each recipe ingredient is gluten free. Products and ingredient sources can change.

Simple Sparkle To toast coconut, spread in ungreased shallow pan. Bake uncovered at 350°F 5 to 7 minutes, stirring occasionally, until golden brown.

Caramel-Carrot Poke Cake

15 servings | **PREP TIME: 10 Minutes** | **START TO FINISH: 3 Hours 15 Minutes**

1 box carrot cake mix with pudding

1 cup water

½ cup butter, melted

3 eggs

1 jar (16 to 17.5 oz) caramel or butterscotch topping

1 container vanilla creamy ready-to-spread frosting

1 Heat oven to 350°F. Grease bottom only of 13 × 9-inch pan with shortening or cooking spray.

2 In large bowl, beat cake mix, water, butter and eggs with electric mixer on low speed 30 seconds, then on medium speed 2 minutes. Pour into pan.

3 Bake 31 to 36 minutes or until toothpick inserted in center comes out clean. Cool 15 minutes. With handle of wooden spoon (¼ to ½ inch diameter), poke holes halfway down into cake every inch, wiping spoon handle occasionally to reduce sticking if necessary.

4 Reserve ½ cup caramel topping. Pour remaining caramel topping over cake; spread evenly over surface, working back and forth to fill holes. Let stand about 15 minutes or until caramel topping has been absorbed into cake. Run knife around side of pan to loosen cake. Cover and refrigerate about 2 hours or until chilled.

5 Set aside 2 tablespoons of the reserved ½ cup caramel topping. Stir remaining topping into frosting; spread over top of cake. Drizzle with reserved 2 tablespoons caramel topping. Cover and refrigerate any remaining cake.

Sweet Secret Forget the frosting! You can use Sweetened Whipped Cream (page 6) or an 8-ounce container of frozen whipped topping, thawed, instead.

Sweet Secret Some caramel toppings are thicker and stickier than others. If the type you purchased is too thick to pour, warm it in the microwave just until it's pourable.

1 Serving: Calories 380; Total Fat 13g (Saturated Fat 6g, Trans Fat 2g); Cholesterol 60mg; Sodium 430mg; Total Carbohydrate 63g (Dietary Fiber 0g); Protein 3g **Exchanges:** 1 Starch, 3 Other Carbohydrate, 2½ Fat **Carbohydrate Choices:** 4

Lemon-Zucchini Pound Cake

16 servings | **PREP TIME: 30 Minutes** | **START TO FINISH: 2 Hours 45 Minutes**

CAKE

3	cups all-purpose flour
1	teaspoon baking powder
¼	teaspoon baking soda
¼	teaspoon salt
1	cup butter, softened
2	cups powdered sugar
4	eggs
⅔	cup milk
2	teaspoons grated lemon peel
2	tablespoons lemon juice
1	cup shredded zucchini (about 1 medium), squeezed to drain

GLAZE

1	cup powdered sugar
1	tablespoon butter, softened
1	tablespoon half-and-half
1	teaspoon grated lemon peel
2	tablespoons lemon juice

Simple Sparkle Top glaze with thin ribbons of lemon zest for a quick, pretty garnish.

1 Heat oven to 350°F. Grease 12-cup fluted tube cake pan with shortening; lightly flour.

2 In medium bowl, mix flour, baking powder, baking soda and salt. In large bowl, beat 1 cup butter with electric mixer on medium speed about 2 minutes or until creamy. Beat in 2 cups powdered sugar. Add eggs, one at a time, beating well after each addition. Reduce speed to low. Add flour mixture alternately with milk, beating well after each addition. Stir in 2 teaspoons lemon peel, 2 tablespoons lemon juice and the zucchini. Spoon batter into pan.

3 Bake 50 to 60 minutes or until toothpick inserted in center comes out clean. Cool 15 minutes; remove from pan to cooling rack. Cool completely, about 1 hour.

4 Meanwhile, in 1-quart saucepan, heat glaze ingredients over medium heat just to boiling, stirring constantly. Remove from heat. Let stand 30 minutes. Drizzle glaze over cake.

1 Serving: Calories 310; Total Fat 14g (Saturated Fat 7g, Trans Fat 0.5g); Cholesterol 85mg; Sodium 190mg; Total Carbohydrate 42g (Dietary Fiber 0g); Protein 5g **Exchanges:** 2 Starch, 1 Other Carbohydrate, 2 Fat **Carbohydrate Choices:** 3

Slow-Cooker Carrot-Zucchini Cake

12 servings | **PREP TIME: 20 Minutes** | **START TO FINISH: 6 Hours 30 Minutes**

CAKE

2	cups Easy Scratch Cake Mix (page 7)
¾	cup vegetable oil
2	tablespoons honey
1	teaspoon ground cinnamon
2	eggs
1	cup finely shredded carrots (about 4 oz)
½	cup shredded zucchini (about 3 oz), squeezed to drain
½	cup sweetened dried cranberries

HONEY BUTTER GLAZE

1	tablespoon butter, softened
1	tablespoon honey
½	cup powdered sugar
¼	teaspoon vanilla
2 to 3	teaspoons milk
	Grated carrot, if desired
	Additional sweetened dried cranberries, if desired

1 Line bottom and sides of 4-quart slow cooker with 1 piece of cooking parchment paper; trim edges if needed. Spray with cooking spray.

2 In large bowl, beat cake mix, oil, honey, cinnamon and eggs with electric mixer on low speed 30 seconds, scraping bowl frequently. Beat on medium speed 3 minutes, scraping bowl occasionally. Stir in carrots, zucchini and cranberries. Spread batter evenly in slow cooker.

3 Place folded, clean dish towel under cover of cooker. Cook on Low heat setting 3 hours 45 minutes to 4 hours, carefully rotating slow cooker's ceramic insert 180 degrees (leaving cover on) after every 45 minutes or until toothpick inserted in center comes out clean. Uncover and transfer ceramic insert from slow cooker to cooling rack. Let stand 10 minutes.

4 Using parchment paper, carefully lift cake out of ceramic insert and transfer to cooling rack. Cool completely, about 2 hours. Remove parchment paper.

5 In small bowl, stir together butter and honey until smooth. Stir in powdered sugar and vanilla. Stir in milk, 1 teaspoon at a time, until of desired consistency. Spread over cake. Garnish with carrot and cranberries.

1 Serving: Calories 300; Total Fat 16g (Saturated Fat 3g, Trans Fat 0g); Cholesterol 35mg; Sodium 125mg; Total Carbohydrate 38g (Dietary Fiber 1g); Protein 2g **Exchanges:** ½ Starch, 2 Other Carbohydrate, 3 Fat **Carbohydrate Choices:** 2½

Sweet Secret If you don't have cranberries, substitute raisins or currants instead.

Sweet Secret Don't be tempted to add extra carrots or zucchini to this cake because the moisture in the cake is sensitive. Paper towels work well to remove excess moisture from the zucchini.

Gluten-Free Zucchini-Devil's Food Snack Cake

12 servings | **PREP TIME: 15 Minutes** | **START TO FINISH: 1 Hour 5 Minutes**

CAKE

- 1 box gluten-free devil's food cake mix
- ½ cup butter, softened
- 1 cup shredded unpeeled zucchini (about 1 medium)
- ½ teaspoon ground cinnamon
- ⅛ teaspoon ground cloves
- ⅓ cup water
- 3 eggs

STREUSEL

- ¼ cup packed brown sugar
- 2 tablespoons butter, softened
- ¼ cup chopped walnuts or pecans

1 Heat oven to 350°F. Grease bottom only of 8- or 9-inch square pan with shortening or cooking spray (without flour).

2 Reserve ¼ cup cake mix for streusel. In large bowl, beat remaining cake mix, ½ cup butter, the zucchini, cinnamon, cloves, water and eggs on low speed 30 seconds. Beat on medium speed 2 minutes, scraping bowl occasionally. Spread in pan.

3 In small bowl, mix streusel ingredients with fork until mixture is crumbly. Sprinkle over batter.

4 Bake in 8-inch pan 44 to 49 minutes, 9-inch pan 38 to 43 minutes, or until toothpick inserted in center comes out clean. Serve warm or cool.

1 Serving: Calories 270; Total Fat 13g (Saturated Fat 7g, Trans Fat 0g); Cholesterol 80mg; Sodium 290mg; Total Carbohydrate 35g (Dietary Fiber 1g); Protein 3g **Exchanges:** ½ Starch, 2 Other Carbohydrate, 2½ Fat **Carbohydrate Choices:** 2

Sweet Secret This moist, streusel-topped cake is very portable, making it perfect for potlucks, picnics or anytime you want to share a homemade treat.

Cooking Gluten Free? Always read labels to make sure each recipe ingredient is gluten free. Products and ingredient sources can change.

Zucchini Cake with Cinnamon–Cream Cheese Frosting

12 servings | **PREP TIME: 25 Minutes** | **START TO FINISH: 2 Hours 5 Minutes**

CAKE

1	box yellow cake mix with pudding
¾	cup milk
½	cup butter, melted
3	eggs
2	teaspoons ground cinnamon
½	teaspoon ground ginger
¼	teaspoon ground nutmeg
2	cups coarsely shredded zucchini (about 2 medium)
¾	cup chopped walnuts

FROSTING

1	package (8 oz) cream cheese, softened
¼	cup butter, softened
1	teaspoon ground cinnamon
1	teaspoon vanilla
1½	cups powdered sugar

1 Heat oven to 350°F. Grease bottom only of 13 × 9-inch pan with shortening or cooking spray.

2 In large bowl, beat cake mix, milk, ½ cup melted butter, the eggs, 2 teaspoons cinnamon, the ginger and nutmeg with electric mixer on medium speed 2 minutes. Stir in zucchini and walnuts. Pour batter into pan.

3 Bake 35 to 40 minutes or until toothpick inserted in center comes out clean. Remove from oven to cooling rack. Cool completely, about 1 hour.

4 In large bowl, beat cream cheese and ¼ cup softened butter with electric mixer on medium-high speed until smooth. Beat in 1 teaspoon cinnamon and the vanilla. On low speed, beat in powdered sugar until frosting is smooth and creamy. Spread frosting over cake. Cover and refrigerate any remaining cake.

1 Serving: Calories 269; Total Fat 21g (Saturated Fat 11.5g, Trans Fat 0.5g); Cholesterol 99mg; Sodium 97mg; Total Carbohydrate 18g (Dietary Fiber 1g); Protein 4g **Exchanges:** 1½ Starch, 2 Other Carbohydrate, 5 Fat **Carbohydrate Choices:** 3

Sweet Secret Zucchini typically isn't peeled when used in baking—just go ahead and shred!

Sweet Secret Short on time? Substitute a container of cream cheese creamy ready-to-spread frosting to frost your cake.

Slow-Cooker Sweet Potato Cake with Brown Sugar Frosting

12 servings | **PREP TIME: 25 Minutes** | **START TO FINISH: 5 Hours 5 Minutes**

CAKE

- 1 cup mashed, cooked sweet potatoes
- ½ cup butter, softened
- ½ cup milk
- 1½ teaspoons vanilla
- 3 eggs
- 3 cups Easy Scratch Cake Mix (page 7)
- 1½ teaspoons pumpkin pie spice
- ⅓ cup raisins
- ⅓ cup chopped pecans

FROSTING

- ¼ cup butter
- ½ cup packed brown sugar
- 2 tablespoons milk
- 1 cup powdered sugar
- 2 tablespoons chopped pecans

1 Line bottom and sides of 4-quart slow cooker with 1 piece of cooking parchment paper; trim edges if needed. Spray with cooking spray.

2 In large bowl, beat sweet potatoes, ½ cup butter, ½ cup milk, the vanilla and eggs with an electric mixer on medium speed 1 minute, scraping bowl frequently, or until blended. Add cake mix and pumpkin pie spice; beat on low speed about 1 minute, scraping bowl occasionally, until dry ingredients are moistened. Fold in raisins and pecans. Spread batter evenly in slow cooker.

3 Place folded, clean dish towel under cover of cooker. Cook on Low heat setting 2 hours 30 minutes to 3 hours 30 minutes, carefully rotating ceramic insert 180 degrees (leaving cover on) after every 45 minutes or until toothpick inserted in center comes out clean. Uncover and transfer ceramic insert from slow cooker to cooling rack. Let stand 10 minutes.

4 Using parchment paper, carefully lift cake out of ceramic insert and transfer to cooling rack. Cool completely, about 1 hour. Remove parchment paper.

5 Meanwhile, in 1-quart saucepan, melt ¼ cup butter over medium heat. Stir in brown sugar. Heat to boiling, stirring constantly. Stir in 2 tablespoons milk. Remove from heat. Cool to lukewarm, about 30 minutes.

6 Gradually stir powdered sugar into butter-sugar mixture in pan with whisk until smooth. Spread over top of cake, allowing excess frosting to drizzle down side of cake. Sprinkle with pecans.

1 Serving: Calories 420; Total Fat 16g (Saturated Fat 8g, Trans Fat 0g); Cholesterol 80mg; Sodium 270mg; Total Carbohydrate 63g (Dietary Fiber 2g); Protein 5g **Exchanges:** 1½ Starch, 2½ Other Carbohydrate, 3 Fat **Carbohydrate Choices:** 4

Sweet Secret You can cook and mash frozen sweet potatoes instead of the fresh sweet potatoes, if you like.

Simple Sparkle Instead of using the brown sugar frosting, top each serving with a spoonful of marshmallow ice-cream topping.

peanut butter, coffee, caramel & turtle cakes

Peanut Butter Tandy Cake

24 servings | **PREP TIME: 20 Minutes** | **START TO FINISH: 1 Hour 35 Minutes**

1 box yellow cake mix with pudding

1¼ cups water

⅓ cup vegetable oil

3 eggs

1½ cups creamy peanut butter

½ cup semisweet chocolate chips

2 tablespoons butter

1 container chocolate creamy ready-to-spread frosting

1 Heat oven to 350°F. Grease bottom and sides of 15 × 10 × 1-inch pan with shortening; lightly flour, or spray with baking spray with flour.

2 In large bowl, beat cake mix, water, oil and eggs with electric mixer on low speed 30 seconds. Beat on medium speed 2 minutes, scraping bowl occasionally. Pour into pan.

3 Bake 22 to 28 minutes or until toothpick inserted in center comes out clean. Cool in pan on cooling rack 30 minutes.

4 In small microwavable bowl, microwave peanut butter uncovered on High 20 seconds or until softened and spreadable. Drop by teaspoonfuls onto surface of warm cake; spread carefully to cover top. Refrigerate cake about 15 minutes or until peanut butter hardens.

5 Meanwhile, in medium microwavable bowl, microwave chocolate chips and butter uncovered on High 30 seconds. Stir; microwave 10 to 20 seconds longer, stirring after 10 seconds, until chips are melted. Stir in frosting. Spread over peanut butter layer.

1 Serving: Calories 330; Total Fat 18g (Saturated Fat 5g, Trans Fat 1.5g); Cholesterol 30mg; Sodium 280mg; Total Carbohydrate 35g (Dietary Fiber 1g); Protein 5g **Exchanges:** ½ Starch, 2 Other Carbohydrate, ½ High-Fat Meat, 2½ Fat **Carbohydrate Choices:** 2

Sweet Secret "Tandy Kake," a white cake made with peanut butter and chocolate, was popular in the 1930s. This is our version.

Sweet Secret For a flavor reminiscent of a popular candy bar, substitute milk chocolate chips for the semisweet.

Candy Bar–Peanut Butter Cake

8 servings | **PREP TIME: 15 Minutes** | **START TO FINISH: 1 Hour**

1½ cups all-purpose flour

¾ cup sugar

⅓ cup peanut butter

¼ cup butter, softened

¾ cup milk

2 teaspoons baking powder

¼ teaspoon salt

2 eggs

½ cup coarsely chopped 1-inch chocolate-covered peanut butter cup candies

1 Heat oven to 350°F. Grease bottom and sides of 8-inch square pan with shortening; lightly flour.

2 In medium bowl, beat all ingredients except candies with electric mixer on low speed 30 seconds, scraping bowl constantly. Beat on high speed 3 minutes, scraping bowl occasionally. Pour into pan. Sprinkle with candies.

3 Bake 35 to 40 minutes or until toothpick inserted in center comes out clean. Serve warm or cool.

1 Serving: Calories 410; Total Fat 19g (Saturated Fat 7g, Trans Fat 0g); Cholesterol 65mg; Sodium 390mg; Total Carbohydrate 50g (Dietary Fiber 2g); Protein 9g **Exchanges:** 2 Starch, 1½ Other Carbohydrate, ½ Medium-Fat Meat, 3 Fat **Carbohydrate Choices:** 3

Sweet Secret If you prefer to use a 9-inch round pan, just follow the recipe as directed and pour batter into 9-inch round pan; bake as directed.

Chocolate–Peanut Butter Candy Cupcakes

24 cupcakes | PREP TIME: 25 Minutes | START TO FINISH: 1 Hour 25 Minutes

1   box triple chocolate fudge cake mix with pudding

1¼   cups water

½   cup vegetable oil

3   eggs

1   bag (8 oz) unwrapped miniature chocolate-covered peanut butter cup candies

2   cups powdered sugar

2   cups creamy peanut butter

¾   cup butter, softened

1   teaspoon vanilla

⅔   cup whipping cream

1 Heat oven to 350°F. Place paper baking cup in each of 24 regular-size muffin cups.

2 In large bowl, beat cake mix, water, oil and eggs with electric mixer on low speed 30 seconds, then on medium speed 2 minutes. Reserve 12 of the peanut butter cup candies for garnish. Coarsely chop remaining candies; stir into batter. Divide batter evenly among muffin cups.

3 Bake 18 minutes or until toothpick inserted in center comes out clean. Cool 10 minutes; remove from pans to cooling racks. Cool completely, about 30 minutes.

4 In medium bowl, beat powdered sugar, peanut butter, butter and vanilla with electric mixer on medium speed until smooth. Add whipping cream; beat until frosting is smooth and spreadable. Frost cupcakes. Cut reserved peanut butter cup candies in half; garnish each cupcake with 1 half candy.

1 Cupcake: Calories 355; Total Fat 22g (Saturated Fat 8g, Trans Fat 0g); Cholesterol 20mg; Sodium 163mg; Total Carbohydrate 39g (Dietary Fiber 3g); Protein 7g **Exchanges:** ½ Starch, 2 Other Carbohydrate, 1 High-Fat Meat, 4 Fat **Carbohydrate Choices:** 2½

Gooey Chocolate–Peanut Butter Cake

20 servings | **PREP TIME: 25 Minutes** | **START TO FINISH: 1 Hour 45 Minutes**

1 box devil's food cake mix with pudding

½ cup butter, softened

2 tablespoons milk

1 egg

1 cup peanut butter chips (from 10-oz bag)

½ cup chopped roasted peanuts

1 package (8 oz) cream cheese, softened

½ cup peanut butter

1 teaspoon vanilla

3 eggs

3¾ cups powdered sugar

Hot fudge topping, if desired

Chopped peanuts, if desired

1 Heat oven to 350°F. Lightly spray 13 × 9-inch pan with baking spray with flour (do not use dark or nonstick pan).

2 In large bowl, mix cake mix, butter, milk and 1 egg with spoon until dough forms. Spoon into pan. Place plastic wrap on dough; press evenly in pan. Remove plastic wrap. Sprinkle dough with peanut butter chips and peanuts.

3 Wipe bowl with paper towel. In same bowl, beat cream cheese, peanut butter, vanilla and 3 eggs with electric mixer on medium speed until smooth. Beat in powdered sugar on low speed. Pour mixture over chocolate mixture in pan; spread evenly.

4 Bake 45 to 50 minutes or until topping is set and deep golden brown. Cool at least 30 minutes to serve warm, or cool completely. When cutting serving pieces, wipe knife with paper towel after cutting each row. Top each piece with hot fudge topping and chopped peanuts. Store covered in refrigerator.

1 Serving: Calories 330; Total Fat 15g (Saturated Fat 7g, Trans Fat 0g); Cholesterol 65mg; Sodium 300mg; Total Carbohydrate 42g (Dietary Fiber 1g); Protein 5g **Exchanges:** 1½ Starch, 1½ Other Carbohydrate, 3 Fat **Carbohydrate Choices:** 3

Sweet Secret Southern cooks have been making ooey-gooey butter cakes for generations. This version uses popular chocolate and peanut butter flavors.

Slow-Cooker Peanut Butter Cup Swirl Cake

12 servings | **PREP TIME: 20 Minutes** | **START TO FINISH: 3 Hours 45 Minutes**

CAKE

1	box yellow cake mix with pudding
1	cup water
3	eggs
½	cup creamy peanut butter
⅓	cup butter, softened
½	cup chocolate-flavor syrup

GLAZE

3	tablespoons creamy peanut butter
2 to 3	tablespoons milk
1	cup powdered sugar

GARNISH

2	tablespoons chocolate-flavor syrup
20	miniature chocolate-covered peanut butter cup candies, unwrapped, cut in half

1 Line bottom and sides of 5½- to 6-quart slow cooker with 1 piece of cooking parchment paper; trim edges if needed. Spray with cooking spray.

2 In large bowl, beat cake mix, water, eggs, ½ cup peanut butter and the butter with electric mixer on low speed 30 seconds, then on medium speed 2 minutes, scraping bowl occasionally. Remove ⅔ cup of the batter to medium bowl; stir in ½ cup chocolate syrup to make chocolate fudge batter.

3 Spoon one-half of the peanut butter batter into slow cooker. Spoon all of the chocolate fudge batter over peanut butter batter. Top with remaining peanut butter batter. Swirl with a knife in a circular motion.

4 Place folded, clean dish towel under cover of cooker. Cook on High setting 1 hour 45 minutes to 2 hours 15 minutes, carefully rotating slow cooker's ceramic insert 180 degrees (leaving cover on) after every 45 minutes or until toothpick inserted in center comes out clean. Uncover and transfer ceramic insert from slow cooker to cooling rack. Let stand 10 minutes. Place cooling rack upside down over insert; turn rack and insert over; remove insert. Cool on cooling rack 1 hour.

5 In medium bowl, beat 3 tablespoons peanut butter and 2 tablespoons milk with whisk until smooth. Add powdered sugar; mix until smooth. If too thick, gradually add additional 1 tablespoon milk until glaze is desired consistency. Spread peanut butter glaze over cake. Drizzle with chocolate syrup. Sprinkle peanut butter cups over top of cake.

1 Serving: Calories 460; Total Fat 20g (Saturated Fat 8g, Trans Fat 0g); Cholesterol 60mg; Sodium 450mg; Total Carbohydrate 62g (Dietary Fiber 2g); Protein 8g **Exchanges:** 1 Starch, 3 Other Carbohydrate, ½ High-Fat Meat, 3 Fat **Carbohydrate Choices:** 4

Banana, Peanut Butter and Marshmallow Poke Cake

12 servings | **PREP TIME: 30 Minutes** | **START TO FINISH: 2 Hours 10 Minutes**

CAKE

- 1 box yellow cake mix with pudding
- 1 cup mashed very ripe bananas (2 medium)
- ½ cup water
- ⅓ cup vegetable oil
- 4 eggs

FILLING

- 1 box (6-serving size) vanilla instant pudding and pie filling mix
- 3 cups cold milk
- ⅓ cup creamy peanut butter

TOPPING

- 1 jar (7 oz) marshmallow creme
- 1 cup butter, softened
- 2 cups powdered sugar
- ⅓ cup creamy peanut butter
- 2 medium bananas, sliced

1 Heat oven to 350°F. Grease bottom only of 13 × 9-inch pan with shortening or cooking spray.

2 In large bowl, beat cake ingredients with electric mixer on low speed 30 seconds, then on medium speed 2 minutes, scraping bowl occasionally. Pour into pan.

3 Bake 26 to 33 minutes or until toothpick inserted in center comes out clean. Remove cake to cooling rack; cool 5 minutes. With handle of wooden spoon (¼ to ½ inch diameter), poke holes halfway down into cake every inch, wiping spoon handle occasionally to reduce sticking if necessary.

4 In large bowl, beat filling ingredients with whisk 1 minute (mixture will thicken). Pour over cake; spread evenly over surface, working back and forth to fill holes. (Some filling should remain on top of cake.) Refrigerate 1 hour.

5 Spoon marshmallow creme into large microwavable bowl. Microwave uncovered on High 15 to 20 seconds to soften. Add softened butter; beat with electric mixer on medium speed until smooth. Beat in powdered sugar until smooth. Spread evenly over cake.

6 Just before serving, in small microwavable bowl, microwave ⅓ cup peanut butter uncovered on High in 15-second intervals until thin enough to drizzle. Top cake with sliced bananas; drizzle with warm peanut butter. Cover and refrigerate any remaining cake.

1 Serving: Calories 680; Total Fat 33g (Saturated Fat 14g, Trans Fat 0.5g); Cholesterol 110mg; Sodium 620mg; Total Carbohydrate 86g (Dietary Fiber 2g); Protein 9g **Exchanges:** 3 Starch, 2½ Other Carbohydrate, 6½ Fat **Carbohydrate Choices:** 6

Sweet Secret If you don't think you'll be serving the entire cake at one time, go ahead and garnish individual slices with the bananas and peanut butter drizzle. This helps to prevent the bananas from browning after they've been sliced.

Simple Sparkle Chopped roasted peanuts also make a lovely garnish instead of the peanut butter drizzle.

Crunchy-Topped Peanut Butter Cake

16 servings | **PREP TIME: 30 Minutes** | **START TO FINISH: 3 Hours 55 Minutes**

CAKE

1	cup coarsely chopped honey-roasted peanuts
2	cups all-purpose flour
1¼	cups sugar
2½	teaspoons baking powder
½	teaspoon salt
½	cup butter, softened
¾	cup creamy peanut butter
3	eggs
⅔	cup milk
1	teaspoon vanilla

GLAZE

½	cup semisweet chocolate chips (3 oz)
2	tablespoons butter
2	tablespoons light corn syrup
1 to 2	teaspoons hot water
3	tablespoons creamy peanut butter

1 Heat oven to 325°F. Grease 12-cup fluted tube cake pan with shortening; lightly flour. Sprinkle nuts evenly in bottom of pan.

2 In medium bowl, mix flour, sugar, baking powder and salt; set aside. In large bowl, beat ½ cup butter and ¾ cup peanut butter with electric mixer on medium speed until smooth, scraping bowl occasionally. Beat in eggs. On low speed, beat in milk and vanilla. Beat in flour mixture just until blended, scraping bowl occasionally. Spread in pan.

3 Bake 55 to 65 minutes or until toothpick inserted in center comes out clean. Cool 10 minutes; remove from pan to cooling rack. Cool completely, about 2 hours.

4 In 1-quart saucepan, heat chocolate chips, 2 tablespoons butter and the corn syrup over low heat, stirring frequently, until chocolate chips are melted. Cool about 10 minutes. Stir in hot water, 1 teaspoon at a time, until glaze is smooth and has the consistency of thick syrup. Spoon over top of cake, allowing glaze to run down side.

5 In small microwavable bowl, microwave 3 tablespoons peanut butter on High 20 seconds or until it can be stirred smooth and is drizzling consistency. Drizzle over top of chocolate glaze.

1 Serving: Calories 390; Total Fat 22g (Saturated Fat 8g, Trans Fat 0g); Cholesterol 55mg; Sodium 330mg; Total Carbohydrate 39g (Dietary Fiber 2g); Protein 9g **Exchanges:** 2½ Other Carbohydrate, 1½ High-Fat Meat, 2 Fat **Carbohydrate Choices:** 2½

Sweet Secret Test the cake in the center, in a crack if there is one, as the crust can clean off the toothpick as you remove it, making you think the cake is done when it might not be.

PB&J Cupcakes

24 cupcakes | **PREP TIME: 25 Minutes** | **START TO FINISH: 1 Hour 25 Minutes**

CUPCAKES

1	box yellow cake mix with pudding
1¼	cups water
¾	cup creamy peanut butter
¼	cup vegetable oil
3	eggs

FROSTING

1	container vanilla whipped ready-to-spread frosting
½	cup creamy peanut butter
2 to 4	tablespoons grape jelly

1 Heat oven to 375°F. Place paper baking cup in each of 24 regular-size muffin cups.

2 In large bowl, beat cupcake ingredients with electric mixer on low speed 30 seconds. Beat on medium speed 2 minutes, scraping bowl occasionally. Divide batter evenly among muffin cups.

3 Bake 15 to 20 minutes or until toothpick inserted in center comes out clean. Cool 10 minutes; remove from pans to cooling racks. Cool completely, about 30 minutes.

4 In medium bowl, mix frosting and ½ cup peanut butter. Frost cupcakes. Make small indentation in center of frosting on each cupcake with back of spoon. Just before serving, spoon ¼ to ½ teaspoon jelly into each indentation.

1 Cupcake: Calories 265; Total Fat 14g (Saturated Fat 3g, Trans Fat 0g); Cholesterol 0mg; Sodium 227mg; Total Carbohydrate 31g (Dietary Fiber 1g); Protein 5g **Exchanges:** ½ Starch, 1½ Other Carbohydrate, ½ High-Fat Meat, 2 Fat **Carbohydrate Choices:** 2

Sweet Secret No grape jelly on the shelf? Substitute your favorite flavor of jam, preserves or jelly.

Sweet Secret Use jelly or jam from a squeezable container to make quick work of adding it to the frosting.

Sweet Secret If you have only one pan and a recipe calls for more cupcakes than your pan will make, cover and refrigerate the rest of the batter while baking the first batch. Cool the pan about 15 minutes, then bake the rest of the batter, adding 1 to 2 minutes to the bake time.

Hazelnut–Candy Bar Icebox Cake

8 servings | **PREP TIME: 15 Minutes** | **START TO FINISH: 45 Minutes**

1 package (10.75 oz) frozen pound cake loaf, thawed

¾ cup hazelnut spread with cocoa

½ cup heavy whipping cream

⅓ cup coarsely chopped malted milk balls

1 bar (1.84 oz) milk chocolate–covered nougat and caramel candy, chopped

⅓ cup coarsely chopped chocolate–peanut butter cups

2 tablespoons chocolate-coated candy pieces

1 Remove cake from pan; rinse pan and dry. Cut cake horizontally into thirds. Spread the top of each layer with ¼ cup hazelnut spread; set aside.

2 In small chilled bowl, beat whipping cream with electric mixer on low speed until cream begins to thicken. Gradually increase speed to high and beat just until stiff peaks form; set aside.

3 Place bottom cake layer in pan. Sprinkle with malted milk balls; press gently. Spread half of the whipped cream over candy. Top with middle cake layer. Sprinkle with chopped candy bar; press gently. Spread remaining whipped cream over candy bar. Arrange top cake layer on cake in pan. Arrange peanut butter cups and candy-coated chocolate pieces over top, pressing gently.

4 Cover and refrigerate 30 minutes or until cake is set but no longer than 24 hours. To serve, cut or pull away sides of pan; transfer to serving plate. Cut into slices.

1 Serving: Calories 510; Total Fat 31g (Saturated Fat 12g, Trans Fat 1g); Cholesterol 60mg; Sodium 120mg; Total Carbohydrate 52g (Dietary Fiber 2g); Protein 6g **Exchanges:** 2 Starch, 1½ Other Carbohydrate, 6 Fat **Carbohydrate Choices:** 3½

Sweet Secret You can start with an angel food loaf cake from the bakery instead of the pound cake. If it doesn't come in a disposable pan, use an 8 × 4-inch loaf pan instead and remove the refrigerated cake using 2 long spatulas.

Sweet Secret If you like, make a scratch loaf-shaped Pound Cake (page 256) instead of using the frozen cake.

Simple Sparkle For a bit of indulgence, drizzle warm hot fudge sauce over slices of this cake.

Coffee-Chocolate Marble Cake

18 servings | **PREP TIME: 30 Minutes** | **START TO FINISH: 2 Hours 20 Minutes**

2¼ cups all-purpose flour

1½ teaspoons baking powder

½ teaspoon baking soda

¼ teaspoon salt

1 cup fat-free plain yogurt

1¼ cups granulated sugar

½ cup vegetable oil

½ cup fat-free egg product

½ cup buttermilk

2 teaspoons vanilla

⅓ cup unsweetened baking cocoa

2 tablespoons instant espresso coffee powder or instant coffee granules

½ cup boiling water

1 tablespoon granulated sugar

2 teaspoons instant espresso coffee powder or instant coffee granules

2 teaspoons powdered sugar or unsweetened baking cocoa, or 1 teaspoon of each

1 Heat oven to 350°F. Grease 10-inch fluted tube cake pan with shortening; lightly flour. In large bowl, mix 1¾ cups of the flour, the baking powder, baking soda and salt.

2 In another large bowl, beat yogurt, 1¼ cups granulated sugar, the oil, egg product, buttermilk and vanilla with whisk. Add yogurt mixture to flour mixture; beat with whisk just until combined. In medium bowl, mix ⅓ cup cocoa and 2 tablespoons coffee powder. Add half of the yogurt mixture (about 2 cups) and stir until smooth. Add remaining ½ cup flour to remaining yogurt mixture; stir just until combined.

3 Spoon half of the white batter into pan. Carefully spoon half of the chocolate batter over white batter. Repeat layers.

4 Bake 30 to 35 minutes or until toothpick inserted near center comes out clean. Cool in pan on cooling rack 15 minutes. Remove cake from pan; place on cooling rack over a sheet of waxed paper. Using long wooden skewer, poke holes into cake in several places to about ½ inch from bottom of cake.

5 In small bowl, stir boiling water, 1 tablespoon granulated sugar and 2 teaspoons coffee powder until sugar and coffee are dissolved. Gradually pour coffee mixture evenly over top of cake. Cool completely on cooling rack, about 1 hour. Sprinkle with powdered sugar.

1 Serving: Calories 210; Total Fat 7g (Saturated Fat 0.5g, Trans Fat 0g); Cholesterol 0mg; Sodium 140mg; Total Carbohydrate 33g (Dietary Fiber 1g); Protein 3g **Exchanges:** 1 Starch, 1 Other Carbohydrate, 1½ Fat **Carbohydrate Choices:** 2

Toffee Tiramisu for a Crowd

24 servings | **PREP TIME: 20 Minutes** | **START TO FINISH: 3 Hours 10 Minutes**

1   box pound cake mix

⅔   cup water or milk

¼   cup butter, softened

2   eggs

1½   cups strong brewed coffee (room temperature)

2   cups sugar

1   cup chocolate-flavor syrup

2   packages (8 oz each) cream cheese, softened

4   cups whipping cream

4   bars (1.4 oz each) chocolate-covered English toffee candy, chopped

1 Heat oven to 350°F. Make and bake cake mix as directed on box for 2 (8 × 4-inch) loaf pans, using water, butter and eggs. Cool 10 minutes; remove from pans to cooling racks. Cool completely, about 1 hour.

2 Cut each pound cake into 9 slices. Arrange slices in two 11 × 7-inch (2-quart) glass baking dishes, cutting slices if necessary to cover bottom of dishes. Drizzle coffee over cakes.

3 In large bowl, beat sugar, chocolate syrup and cream cheese with electric mixer on medium speed until smooth. Add whipping cream; beat on medium speed until light and fluffy. Spread over cakes. Sprinkle with chopped toffee candy.

4 Cover; refrigerate at least 1 hour but no longer than 24 hours.

1 Serving: Calories 440; Total Fat 27g (Saturated Fat 16g, Trans Fat 0g); Cholesterol 0mg; Sodium 190mg; Total Carbohydrate 47g (Dietary Fiber 0g); Protein 4g **Exchanges:** ½ Starch, 2½ Other Carbohydrate, 5 Fat **Carbohydrate Choices:** 3

Sweet Secret Chopping the toffee bars is easier if you freeze them first.

Sweet Secret Two 10.75-ounce packages of frozen pound cake, thawed, can be substituted for the pound cake mix; omit the water, butter and eggs and step 1.

Tiramisu

8 servings | **PREP TIME: 35 Minutes** | **START TO FINISH: 5 Hours 35 Minutes**

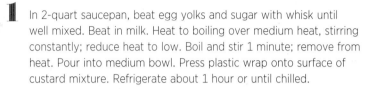

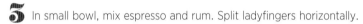

6	egg yolks
¾	cup sugar
⅔	cup milk
2	containers (8 oz each) mascarpone cheese or 2 packages (8 oz each) cream cheese, softened
1¼	cups whipping cream
½	teaspoon vanilla
¼	cup cold brewed espresso or very strong coffee
2	tablespoons rum
2	packages (3 oz each) ladyfingers (24 ladyfingers)
1½	teaspoons unsweetened baking cocoa

1 In 2-quart saucepan, beat egg yolks and sugar with whisk until well mixed. Beat in milk. Heat to boiling over medium heat, stirring constantly; reduce heat to low. Boil and stir 1 minute; remove from heat. Pour into medium bowl. Press plastic wrap onto surface of custard mixture. Refrigerate about 1 hour or until chilled.

2 Add cheese to custard mixture. Beat with electric mixer on medium speed until smooth; set aside. Wash and dry beaters. In chilled large, deep bowl, beat whipping cream and vanilla with electric mixer on low speed until mixture begins to thicken. Gradually increase speed to high and beat until stiff peaks form; set aside.

3 In small bowl, mix espresso and rum. Split ladyfingers horizontally.

4 In ungreased 11 × 7-inch (2-quart) glass baking dish, arrange half of the ladyfingers in single layer. Brush with espresso mixture (do not soak). Spread half of the cheese mixture over ladyfingers; spread with half of the whipped cream. Repeat layers with remaining ladyfingers, espresso mixture, cheese mixture and whipped cream. Sprinkle with cocoa. Cover and refrigerate at least 4 hours to develop flavors but no longer than 24 hours. Store covered in refrigerator.

1 Serving: Calories 540; Total Fat 38g (Saturated Fat 22g, Trans Fat 1.5g); Cholesterol 270mg; Sodium 260mg; Total Carbohydrate 39g (Dietary Fiber 0g); Protein 9g **Exchanges:** 2 Starch, ½ Other Carbohydrate, 7½ Fat **Carbohydrate Choices:** 2½

Sweet Secret Mascarpone has a delicate, buttery flavor with just a hint of sweetness. Look for it in the cheese case in large supermarkets, specialty cheese shops or gourmet food stores.

Sweet Secret If you prefer, ⅛ teaspoon rum extract mixed with 2 tablespoons water can be substituted for the rum.

Sweet Secret You can substitute 2 packages (10.75 ounces each) frozen (thawed) pound cake for the ladyfingers. Place each pound cake on its side; carefully cut each cake into 3 slices. Brush each slice with espresso mixture. Arrange 3 slices crosswise in baking dish. Spread half of the cheese mixture over cake; spread with half of the whipped cream. Repeat layers with remaining pound cake, espresso mixture, cheese mixture and whipped cream.

Mocha Cappuccino Pudding Cake

12 servings | **PREP TIME: 10 Minutes** | **START TO FINISH: 55 Minutes**

1¼ cups all-purpose flour

1¾ cups sugar

¼ cup unsweetened baking cocoa

4 teaspoons instant espresso coffee powder or granules

1½ teaspoons baking powder

½ teaspoon salt

½ cup fat-free (skim) milk

2 tablespoons butter, melted

1 teaspoon vanilla

1½ cups very warm fat-free (skim) milk (120°F to 130°F)

1 Place sheet of foil or cookie sheet on lower oven rack. Heat oven to 350°F.

2 In medium bowl, mix flour, ¾ cup of the sugar, 2 tablespoons of the cocoa, 3 teaspoons of the coffee powder, the baking powder and salt. Stir in ½ cup milk, the melted butter and vanilla until well blended. Spread batter in ungreased 9-inch square pan.

3 In small bowl, mix remaining 1 cup sugar, 2 tablespoons cocoa and 1 teaspoon coffee powder; sprinkle evenly over batter. Pour warm milk over top.

4 Bake on middle oven rack 35 to 45 minutes or until center is set and firm to the touch. Spoon warm cake into dessert dishes.

1 Serving: Calories 220; Total Fat 2.5g (Saturated Fat 1g, Trans Fat 0g); Cholesterol 5mg; Sodium 190mg; Total Carbohydrate 46g (Dietary Fiber 1g); Protein 4g **Exchanges:** 1 Starch, 2 Other Carbohydrate, ½ Fat **Carbohydrate Choices:** 3

Sweet Secret Even though this dessert could be served hot from the oven, let it stand a bit before serving so the pudding isn't too hot to eat, especially for kids.

Caramel-Coffee Poke Cake

15 servings | **PREP TIME: 25 Minutes** | **START TO FINISH: 3 Hours 15 Minutes**

CAKE

- 4 cups Easy Scratch Cake Mix (page 7)
- ½ cup butter, softened
- 1¼ cups milk
- 1 teaspoon vanilla
- 3 eggs

FILLING

- 1 package (8 oz) cream cheese, softened
- ½ cup caramel topping
- ½ cup cold strong coffee
- ¼ cup chopped chocolate-covered espresso beans

FROSTING AND TOPPING

- 3 cups Sweetened Whipped Cream (page 6)
- ¼ cup caramel topping
- 1 cup mini pretzel twists, coarsely crushed
- ¼ cup coarsely chopped chocolate-covered espresso beans

1 Heat oven to 350° F. Grease bottom and sides of 13 × 9-inch pan with shortening or spray with cooking spray.

2 In large bowl, beat cake mix, butter, milk, vanilla and eggs with electric mixer on low speed 30 seconds, scraping bowl occasionally. Beat on medium speed 2 minutes, scraping bowl occasionally, or until light and fluffy. Pour into pan.

3 Bake 30 to 35 minutes or until cake springs back when lightly touched. Cool 15 minutes.

4 With handle of wooden spoon (¼ to ½ inch diameter), poke holes halfway down into cake every inch, wiping spoon handle occasionally to prevent sticking if necessary.

5 In medium bowl, beat cream cheese on low speed 30 seconds. Gradually beat in ½ cup caramel topping and the coffee for 1 minute, scraping bowl occasionally, until smooth and creamy. Stir in espresso beans. Pour cream cheese mixture evenly over surface, working back and forth to fill holes. (Some filling should remain on top of cake.) Cover loosely and refrigerate 2 hours or until chilled.

6 Spread Sweetened Whipped Cream over top of cake; drizzle with ¼ cup caramel topping. Just before serving, top with pretzels and espresso beans. Cover and refrigerate any remaining cake.

1 Serving: Calories 480; Total Fat 24g (Saturated Fat 14g, Trans Fat 0.5g); Cholesterol 105mg; Sodium 410mg; Total Carbohydrate 58g (Dietary Fiber 1g); Protein 6g **Exchanges:** 2 Starch, 2 Other Carbohydrate, 4½ Fat **Carbohydrate Choices:** 4

Sweet Secret Go ahead and make a yellow cake mix instead of the scratch cake; continue as directed in step 3. Use frozen (thawed) whipped topping for the Sweetened Whipped Cream in step 6.

Sweet Secret For cold strong coffee, make double-strength instant coffee or instant espresso. Cool in the refrigerator until ready to use.

Maple-Espresso Cake

16 servings | PREP TIME: 20 Minutes | START TO FINISH: 2 Hours 20 Minutes

2½   cups all-purpose flour

4   teaspoons instant espresso coffee powder or granules

2½   teaspoons baking powder

½   teaspoon baking soda

¼   teaspoon salt

1   cup butter, softened

½   cup packed brown sugar

¾   cup real maple syrup

1   teaspoon vanilla bean paste or vanilla

3   eggs

1¼   cups sour cream

4   oz white chocolate baking squares, melted, cooled

3   tablespoons coffee beans, chopped, if desired

1 Heat oven to 350°F. Grease 12-cup fluted tube cake pan with shortening; lightly flour. In medium bowl, mix flour, espresso powder, baking powder, baking soda and salt.

2 In large bowl, beat butter and brown sugar with electric mixer on medium speed until light and fluffy, about 3 minutes. Add syrup and vanilla bean paste; beat until well blended. Beat in eggs, one at a time, until blended. On low speed, beat in flour mixture alternately with 1 cup of the sour cream. Spoon batter into pan.

3 Bake 45 to 50 minutes or until toothpick inserted in center comes out clean. Cool 10 minutes; remove from pan to cooling rack. Cool completely, about 1 hour.

4 In small bowl, mix melted white chocolate and remaining ¼ cup sour cream. Spoon or pour over cake. Sprinkle with coffee beans.

1 Serving: Calories 320; Total Fat 18g (Saturated Fat 11g, Trans Fat 0g); Cholesterol 0mg; Sodium 300mg; Total Carbohydrate 36g (Dietary Fiber 0g); Protein 4g **Exchanges:** 1 Starch, 1½ Other Carbohydrate, 3½ Fat **Carbohydrate Choices:** 2½

How to Build an Ice-Cream Cake

There are so many reasons to love ice-cream cakes! Whether it's the indulgent concoction of ingredients, the multitude of layers or that you get to have cake and ice cream together, it's a smart dessert to make because they're easy, can be made ahead and are sure to bring smiles.

WHAT'S YOUR CAKE?

The cake for your ice-cream cake may or may not be cake at all! Look at all the options here for your "cake" layer. Start with a fully cooled cake before adding other ingredients:

Single layer cake (prepared or store bought)

Regular, Angel food, Pound cake

You can also split a single layer cake to have two thinner layers by cutting it horizontally in half with a serrated knife. Partially freeze the cake before cutting to have less crumbs.

Brownies, Graham crackers

Crushed cookies mixed with melted butter—about 4 cups crushed cookies to ½ cup melted butter. Press in the bottom of a 13 × 9-inch pan. The butter will make the cookie layer set up when frozen.

Snack cakes, Doughnuts, Ice-cream sandwiches

Get creative with delicious treats from your grocery store or bakery.

SIMPLE LAYERS

Make your ice-cream cake stand out with a few simple layers. Add these in one or more layers to your stand-out cake:

- **Caramel sauce**
- **Chocolate sauce** (stays soft) **or fudge topping** (holds its shape when frozen)
- **Chopped nuts or candy bars**—For chewy candy
- **Crushed cookies or hard candies**

- **Jelly or jam**—These are fairly easy to spread; preserves typically have too much fruit to make them spreadable.
- **Sprinkles**

ICE CREAM

Use just one ice cream flavor, or mix and match ice cream, sherbet and frozen yogurt for fun flavor and color combinations.

- Soften ice cream slightly before spreading, either on the counter at room temperature or using your microwave if it has a button for softening ice cream.
- For even more texture and flavor, add chopped fruit, nuts, crumbled cookies or chopped candy bars to the softened ice cream before spreading on the cake.
- You may need to allow the frozen ice-cream cake to soften again before serving so it's easier to cut and eat.

TOPPING

Finish off the top of your ice-cream cake like a pro! Add one or more of the following:

- Fudge topping layer with whipped cream dollops sprinkled with toasted coconut or finely chopped nuts
- Sweetened Whipped Cream (page 6) with sprinkles, chopped candy bars or crushed cookies.

ONE MORE LAYER

Serve pieces of your ice-cream cake drizzled with chocolate sauce or fudge, caramel or butterscotch topping. Or drizzle with one kind and then drizzle with another! (Can you ever have too much?)

Candy Bar Ice-Cream Cake 'Wiches

16 servings | **PREP TIME: 25 Minutes** | **START TO FINISH: 6 Hours 35 Minutes**

FILLING

1½ cups chopped milk chocolate–covered peanut, caramel and nougat candy bars (about four 1.75- to 2-oz bars)

1.5 to 1.75 quarts chocolate ice cream, softened (about 6 cups)

CAKE

¼ cup decorator sprinkles

2 cups Easy Scratch Cake Mix (page 7)

⅔ cup milk

¼ cup butter, softened

½ teaspoon vanilla

1 egg

1 Line 9-inch square pan with plastic wrap, allowing wrap to extend over edges. In large bowl, fold candy bars into ice cream until blended. Spread evenly in pan. Freeze 3 to 4 hours or until firm.

2 Meanwhile, heat oven to 350°F. Line bottom of another 9-inch square pan with parchment paper. Sprinkle half of the sprinkles evenly over bottom of pan. In medium bowl, beat cake mix, milk, butter, vanilla and egg on low speed 30 seconds, scraping bowl occasionally. Beat on medium speed 2 minutes or until fluffy. Pour into pan. Sprinkle with remaining sprinkles.

3 Bake 23 to 28 minutes or until cake springs back when lightly touched. Run knife around sides of pan. Cool in pan 10 minutes. Remove from pan to cooling rack. Cool completely, about 30 minutes.

4 Slice cake horizontally in half; remove top half of cake. Unwrap ice cream; place on cut side of bottom of cake. Place top of cake, cut side down, on ice cream. Cut into 4 rows by 4 rows. Quickly wrap each sandwich in plastic wrap. Freeze at least 1 hour or until firm but no longer than 1 month.

1 Serving: Calories 370; Total Fat 17g (Saturated Fat 11g, Trans Fat 0g); Cholesterol 45mg; Sodium 160mg; Total Carbohydrate 48g (Dietary Fiber 2g); Protein 5g **Exchanges:** 2 Starch, 1 Other Carbohydrate, 3 Fat **Carbohydrate Choices:** 3

Sweet Secret To use the same 9-inch pan for both freezing and baking, freeze ice cream until firm. Remove from pan and return ice cream to freezer.

Sweet Secret Omit making the scratch cake by starting with a yellow cake mix. Make as directed using 1¼ cups water, ½ cup softened butter and 2 eggs. Pour half of the batter into square pan. Use remaining batter for another purpose, such as cupcakes or a round cake.

Turtle Ice-Cream Cake

12 servings | **PREP TIME: 20 Minutes** | **START TO FINISH: 11 Hours**

10 chocolate wafer cookies, finely crushed (½ cup)

1 tablespoon butter, melted

3 cups chocolate ice cream, slightly softened

½ cup hot fudge topping

⅔ cup chopped pecans

3 cups vanilla ice cream, slightly softened

¼ cup caramel topping

1 In small bowl, mix cookie crumbs and butter until crumbly. Press gently and evenly in bottom of ungreased 9-inch springform pan. Freeze 30 minutes.

2 Drop chocolate ice cream by small spoonfuls over crust; carefully spread until smooth. Freeze 1 hour or until firm.

3 Spoon and carefully spread hot fudge topping over chocolate ice cream. Sprinkle with ⅓ cup of the pecans; press lightly. Freeze 1 hour or until firm.

4 Drop vanilla ice cream by small spoonfuls over pecan layer; carefully spread until smooth. Sprinkle with remaining ⅓ cup pecans. Cover; freeze at least 8 hours or overnight.

5 Let stand at room temperature 5 to 10 minutes before serving. Carefully remove side of pan. Cut dessert into 12 wedges. Place on individual dessert plates. Drizzle each with 1 teaspoon of the caramel topping. Store covered in freezer.

1 Serving: Calories 280; Total Fat 14g (Saturated Fat 6g, Trans Fat 0g); Cholesterol 30mg; Sodium 160mg; Total Carbohydrate 34g (Dietary Fiber 2g); Protein 4g **Exchanges:** 1½ Starch, 1 Other Carbohydrate, 2½ Fat **Carbohydrate Choices:** 2

Sweet Secret Be sure to drop the ice cream by small spoonfuls so that spreading it is minimal and you don't disturb the preceding layers.

Sweet Secret Pecans are traditional for turtle desserts, but walnuts or cashews are just as delicious.

Easy Turtle Cake with Broiled Coconut Frosting

9 servings | **PREP TIME: 20 Minutes** | **START TO FINISH: 2 Hours 15 Minutes**

CAKE

- ¼ cup butter, softened
- 2 cups Easy Scratch Cake Mix (page 7)
- ¾ cup milk
- 1 teaspoon vanilla
- 2 eggs
- ¼ cup chopped pecans
- ½ cup miniature semisweet chocolate chips

COCONUT FROSTING

- ¾ cup coconut
- ⅓ cup chopped pecans
- ⅓ cup packed brown sugar
- ¼ cup cold butter
- ½ cup caramel topping

1 Heat oven to 350°F. Grease 8-inch square pan with shortening; lightly flour.

2 In large bowl, beat butter, cake mix, milk, vanilla and eggs with electric mixer on low speed 30 seconds, scraping bowl constantly. Beat on medium speed 2 minutes, scraping bowl occasionally until well mixed. Stir in ¼ cup pecans. Pour batter into pan. Sprinkle with chocolate chips.

3 Bake 35 to 40 minutes or until toothpick inserted in center comes out clean. Cool 10 minutes.

4 Meanwhile, in small bowl, mix coconut, ⅓ cup pecans and the brown sugar until well mixed. Using fork, cut butter into coconut mixture until crumbly. Sprinkle evenly over cake. Set oven control to broil. Broil cake with top 3 inches from heat about 2 minutes or until bubbly and golden brown. Cool 1 hour. Drizzle with caramel topping.

1 Serving: Calories 480; Total Fat 22g (Saturated Fat 12g, Trans Fat 0g); Cholesterol 70mg; Sodium 320mg; Total Carbohydrate 63g (Dietary Fiber 2g); Protein 5g **Exchanges:** 2 Starch, 2 Other Carbohydrate, 4 Fat **Carbohydrate Choices:** 4

Sweet Secret Chopped walnuts or almonds can be substituted for the chopped pecans in this recipe.

Simple Sparkle For a more decadent dessert, top with a dollop of whipped cream before drizzling with caramel topping.

Chocolate Turtle Cake

20 servings | **PREP TIME: 25 Minutes** | **START TO FINISH: 1 Hour 50 Minutes**

1 box devil's food cake mix with pudding

1¼ cups water

½ cup vegetable oil

3 eggs

1 bag (14 oz) caramels

½ cup evaporated milk

1 cup chopped pecans

1 cup semisweet chocolate chips (6 oz)

Caramel and chocolate toppings, if desired

Chopped pecans, if desired

1 Heat oven to 350°F. Grease bottom only of 13 × 9-inch pan with shortening or cooking spray.

2 Make cake batter as directed on box, using water, oil and eggs. Pour half of batter into pan. Bake 22 minutes. Refrigerate remaining batter.

3 Meanwhile, in 1-quart saucepan, heat caramels and evaporated milk over medium heat, stirring frequently, until caramels are melted. Stir in pecans.

4 Pour caramel mixture over warm cake in pan. Sprinkle with chocolate chips. Spread with remaining batter.

5 Bake 25 to 28 minutes longer or until cake springs back when touched lightly in center. Run knife around sides of pan to loosen cake. Cool at least 30 minutes. Drizzle with toppings and sprinkle with pecans. Store cake loosely covered.

1 Serving: Calories 310; Total Fat 15g (Saturated Fat 4g, Trans Fat 0g); Cholesterol 35mg; Sodium 250mg; Total Carbohydrate 40g (Dietary Fiber 1g); Protein 4g **Exchanges:** 1 Starch, 1½ Other Carbohydrate, 3 Fat **Carbohydrate Choices:** 2½

Sweet Secret Serve this ooey-gooey cake with your favorite ice cream or whipped cream.

Candy Ice-Cream Cake Bars

20 servings | **PREP TIME: 40 Minutes** | **START TO FINISH: 5 Hours 50 Minutes**

1 box (18.3 oz) fudge brownie mix

½ cup vegetable oil

3 tablespoons water

3 eggs

½ cup chopped cocktail peanuts

¾ cup caramel sauce

1 container (28 oz) chocolate ice cream, softened

1 container (28 oz) dulce de leche caramel ice cream, softened

Sweetened Whipped Cream (page 6)

3 bars (1.86 oz each) milk chocolate–covered peanut, caramel and nougat candy, chopped

2 tablespoons chocolate-flavor syrup

1 Heat oven to 350°F. Grease bottom only of 13 x 9-inch pan with shortening or cooking spray.

2 In large bowl, mix brownie mix, oil, water and eggs until well blended. Stir in peanuts. Pour into pan.

3 Bake 24 to 26 minutes or until toothpick inserted 2 inches from side of pan comes out almost clean. Remove brownie from oven to cooling rack. Cool 30 minutes.

4 Spread ½ cup of the caramel sauce over brownie. Freeze 10 minutes. Evenly spread softened chocolate ice cream over caramel layer. Freeze 1 hour longer.

5 Evenly spread softened caramel ice cream over chocolate ice-cream layer. Cover; freeze 3 hours longer or until firm.

6 When ready to serve, spread whipped cream over frozen cake. Sprinkle with chopped candy bars. Drizzle with remaining ¼ cup caramel sauce and the chocolate syrup. Store covered in freezer.

1 Serving: Calories 426; Total Fat 22g (Saturated Fat 11g, Trans Fat 0.5g); Cholesterol 79mg; Sodium 148mg; Total Carbohydrate 53g (Dietary Fiber 1g); Protein 7g **Exchanges:** 2 Starch, 2 Other Carbohydrate, 5 Fat **Carbohydrate Choices:** 4

Sweet Secret To soften ice cream, remove from freezer to refrigerator 20 to 30 minutes before needed.

Sweet Secret You can substitute 1 container (8 ounces) frozen whipped topping, thawed, for the Sweetened Whipped Cream.

Butterscotch Mug Cake

2 mug cakes | PREP TIME: 5 Minutes | START TO FINISH: 10 Minutes

CAKE

- 3 tablespoons butter
- ¾ cup Easy Brown Sugar Scratch Cake Mix (page 7)
- ¼ cup milk
- 1 tablespoon chopped nuts
- 1 egg

TOPPING

- 2 scoops vanilla ice cream
- 2 tablespoons butterscotch caramel topping

1 Place butter in 2-cup microwavable measure; cover with waxed paper. Microwave on High 2 to 3 minutes or until butter begins to brown. Carefully remove from microwave; let cool slightly. Stir in cake mix, milk, nuts and egg with fork until blended.

2 Divide batter between two microwavable 10-oz or larger mugs. Microwave uncovered on High 1½ to 2 minutes or until toothpick inserted in center comes out clean and cake pulls away from side of mug. Cool 5 minutes.

3 Top each cake with 1 scoop ice cream. Drizzle with butterscotch topping.

1 Mug Cake: Calories 660; Total Fat 30g (Saturated Fat 17g, Trans Fat 1g); Cholesterol 170mg; Sodium 540mg; Total Carbohydrate 87g (Dietary Fiber 2g); Protein 10g **Exchanges:** 1 Starch, 4 Other Carbohydrate, 1 Milk, 4½ Fat **Carbohydrate Choices:** 6

Sweet Secret Add the egg last to keep the hot butter from cooking the egg.

Sweet Secret Substitute miniature chocolate chips for the nuts. Just cool the butter a few minutes before adding the chips to prevent them from melting.

Five-Ingredient Caramel Candy Bar Apple Cake

9 servings | **PREP TIME: 20 Minutes** | **START TO FINISH: 1 Hour**

6 eggs

1 teaspoon vanilla

2 cups Easy Scratch Cake Mix (page 7)

3 cups chopped Granny Smith apples, peeled, chopped (about 2 large)

8 bars (fun-size) chocolate-covered caramel cookie candy, each cut into 8 pieces (about 1 cup)

Additional (fun-size) chocolate-covered caramel cookie candy, chopped, if desired

1 Heat oven to 350°F. Grease bottom and sides of 9-inch square pan with shortening or spray with cooking spray.

2 In medium bowl, beat eggs and vanilla with electric mixer on high speed 3 to 5 minutes, scraping bowl occasionally, or until very thick and lemon-colored. Add cake mix. Beat on medium speed 1 minute, scraping bowl frequently, or until batter is well blended. Fold apples into batter; spread in pan. Sprinkle candies over batter.

3 Bake 35 to 40 minutes or until light golden brown and toothpick inserted in center comes out clean. Serve warm or cool topped with additional chopped candy bars.

1 Serving: Calories 280; Total Fat 7g (Saturated Fat 3.5g, Trans Fat 0g); Cholesterol 125mg; Sodium 200mg; Total Carbohydrate 46g (Dietary Fiber 1g); Protein 6g **Exchanges:** 1 Starch, 2 Other Carbohydrate, ½ Medium-Fat Meat, 1 Fat **Carbohydrate Choices:** 3

Sweet Secret Placing the candies on top of the batter, not in the batter, means they won't sink to the bottom of the cake. Try with your favorite candy bar, using 1 cup of small cut up pieces.

Sweet Secret If you've got a yellow cake mix with pudding on hand, you can use it (dry) in place of the Easy Scratch Cake Mix. Spray bottom and side of 9-inch springform pan with cooking spray. Pour into pan. Bake 45 to 50 minutes or until golden brown and toothpick inserted in center comes out clean. Cool 10 minutes; remove side of pan. Cool 30 minutes longer. Serve warm or cool.

Simple Sparkle If you like, sprinkle the top of the cake lightly with powdered sugar for a dressed-up look. Place a tablespoon of the sugar in a fine-mesh strainer; tap the edge of the strainer with a spoon while moving it over the cake.

chocolate cakes

Slow-Cooker Brownie Pudding Cake

8 servings | PREP TIME: 10 Minutes | START TO FINISH: 3 Hours 10 Minutes

1 cup all-purpose flour

1¼ cups granulated sugar

¼ cup Dutch processed baking cocoa

¼ teaspoon salt

¼ cup vegetable oil

1 teaspoon vanilla

3 egg whites

2 whole eggs

2 oz bittersweet baking chocolate, melted

¼ cup coarsely chopped walnuts, toasted

Powdered sugar, if desired

1 In medium bowl, mix flour, granulated sugar, cocoa and salt. In small bowl, stir oil, vanilla, egg whites and eggs with whisk. Add egg mixture to flour mixture; stir until blended. Stir in melted chocolate. Stir in walnuts.

2 Spray bottom and sides of 3½-quart slow cooker with cooking spray. Pour batter into slow cooker.

3 Place folded, clean dish towel under cover of cooker. Cook on Low heat setting 2 hours to 2 hours 30 minutes, carefully rotating slow cooker's ceramic insert 180 degrees (leaving cover on) after every 45 minutes or until set around edges but still soft in center. Turn off slow cooker. Let stand covered 30 minutes. Sprinkle with powdered sugar.

1 Serving: Calories 340; Total Fat 14g (Saturated Fat 2.5g, Trans Fat 0g); Cholesterol 0mg; Sodium 110mg; Total Carbohydrate 49g (Dietary Fiber 2g); Protein 6g **Exchanges:** 1 Starch, 2 Other Carbohydrate, 2½ Fat **Carbohydrate Choices:** 3

Sweet Secret To toast walnuts, sprinkle in ungreased heavy skillet. Cook over medium heat 5 to 7 minutes, stirring frequently until walnuts begin to brown, then stirring constantly until walnuts are light brown.

Simple Sparkle Turn this cake into brownie sundaes with a scoop of ice cream and a drizzle of chocolate topping.

Vegan Slow-Cooker Fudgy Pudding Cake

8 servings | PREP TIME: 15 Minutes | START TO FINISH: 3 Hours 25 Minutes

1 cup all-purpose flour

½ cup granulated vegan sugar

2 tablespoons unsweetened dark baking cocoa

2 teaspoons baking powder

½ teaspoon salt

½ cup chocolate almond milk

2 tablespoons vegetable oil

1 teaspoon vanilla

¾ cup vegan brown sugar

¼ cup unsweetened dark baking cocoa

1½ cups hot water

1 Spray bottom and sides of 3½-quart slow cooker with cooking spray.

2 In medium bowl, mix flour, granulated sugar, 2 tablespoons cocoa, the baking powder and salt. Stir in almond milk, oil and vanilla until smooth (batter will be thick). Spread batter evenly in bottom of slow cooker.

3 In small bowl, mix brown sugar and ¼ cup cocoa. Stir in hot water until smooth. Pour evenly over batter in slow cooker.

4 Place folded, clean dish towel under cover of cooker. Cook on Low heat setting 2 hours to 2 hours 30 minutes, carefully rotating slow cooker's ceramic insert 180 degrees (leaving cover on) after every 45 minutes or until toothpick inserted in center comes out clean. Uncover and transfer ceramic insert from slow cooker to cooling rack.

5 Let stand 30 to 40 minutes to cool slightly before serving (sauce will thicken as it cools). Spoon warm cake into dessert dishes. Spoon sauce over top.

1 Serving: Calories 250; Total Fat 4.5g (Saturated Fat 0.5g, Trans Fat 0g); Cholesterol 0mg; Sodium 290mg; Total Carbohydrate 49g (Dietary Fiber 2g); Protein 2g **Exchanges:** ½ Starch, 3 Other Carbohydrate, 1 Fat **Carbohydrate Choices:** 3

Sweet Secret You can substitute regular unsweetened baking cocoa for the dark cocoa, but you will see a substantial difference in color.

Sweet Sparkle If you like, serve with vegan frozen dessert (such as vegan frozen ice cream). You'll find it in the freezer section of your grocery store. Many are made using coconut milk and come in a variety of flavors. Add fresh raspberries or strawberries for a splash of color!

Fudge Lover's Cream Cheese Cake

15 servings | **PREP TIME: 30 Minutes** | **START TO FINISH: 2 Hours 25 Minutes**

CAKE

- 1 box yellow or devil's food cake mix with pudding
- 1 box (4-serving size) chocolate instant pudding and pie filling mix
- ¾ cup hot water
- ¾ cup vegetable oil
- 1 teaspoon vanilla
- 4 eggs

FILLING

- 1 package (8 oz) cream cheese, softened
- ½ cup sugar
- 1 egg
- ½ cup semisweet chocolate chips
- ½ cup chopped nuts, if desired

FROSTING

- 1 container vanilla or chocolate creamy ready-to-spread frosting

Simple Sparkle If you're using vanilla frosting, sprinkle the frosted cake with chocolate chips.

1 Heat oven to 350°F. Spray bottom only of 13 x 9-inch pan with baking spray with flour.

2 In large bowl, beat cake ingredients with electric mixer on low speed 30 seconds, then on medium speed 2 minutes, scraping bowl occasionally. Pour into pan.

3 In large bowl, beat cream cheese, sugar and 1 egg with electric mixer on medium speed until smooth and creamy. Stir in chocolate chips. Spoon filling by tablespoonfuls evenly over batter. Using table knife, swirl filling through batter. Sprinkle with nuts.

4 Bake 47 to 55 minutes or until toothpick inserted in center comes out clean. Cool completely, about 1 hour. Spread frosting over cake. Store covered in refrigerator.

1 Serving: Calories 480; Total Fat 25g (Saturated Fat 8g, Trans Fat 2g); Cholesterol 85mg; Sodium 430mg; Total Carbohydrate 61g (Dietary Fiber 1g); Protein 4g **Exchanges:** 1 Starch, 3 Other Carbohydrate, 5 Fat **Carbohydrate Choices:** 4

Gluten-Free Chocolate Chip Ice-Cream Dessert

15 servings | **PREP TIME: 30 Minutes** | **START TO FINISH: 3 Hours 45 Minutes**

1 box gluten-free chocolate chip cookie mix

½ cup butter, softened

1 egg

1 bottle (7.25 oz) chocolate topping that forms hard shell

1 container (1.5 quart) chocolate chip ice cream (6 cups)

1 Heat oven to 350°F. In large bowl, stir cookie mix, butter and egg until soft dough forms. On ungreased cookie sheet, make 5 cookies by dropping dough by tablespoonfuls. Bake 8 to 10 minutes or until edges are golden brown. Cool 2 minutes; remove from cookie sheet to cooling rack.

2 Meanwhile, using moistened fingers (dough will be sticky), press remaining dough in bottom of ungreased 13 × 9-inch pan.

3 Bake 16 to 18 minutes or until set. Cool completely, about 30 minutes.

4 Spread ⅓ cup of the chocolate topping over cooled baked crust. Freeze 10 to 15 minutes or until chocolate is set. Meanwhile, remove ice cream from freezer to soften.

5 Spread softened ice cream evenly over chocolate-topped crust. Crumble 5 baked cookies; sprinkle over ice-cream layer. Drizzle remaining chocolate topping over cookie crumbs. Cover; freeze at least 2 hours or overnight. Remove from freezer 10 minutes before cutting. Store covered in freezer.

1 Serving: Calories 400; Total Fat 21g (Saturated Fat 12g, Trans Fat 0g); Cholesterol 55mg; Sodium 260mg; Total Carbohydrate 51g (Dietary Fiber 0g); Protein 4g **Exchanges:** 1½ Starch, 2 Other Carbohydrate, 4 Fat **Carbohydrate Choices:** 3½

Sweet Secret To make the cake easier to cut, line bottom and sides of pan with foil, leaving foil overhanging at two opposite sides of pan. Spray bottom only of foil-lined pan with cooking spray. Use foil to lift cake out of pan. Pull foil from sides of cake before cutting into serving pieces.

Cooking Gluten Free? Always read labels to make sure each recipe ingredient is gluten free. Products and ingredient sources can change.

Chocolate Chip Snack Cake

9 servings | **PREP TIME: 20 Minutes** | **START TO FINISH: 1 Hour 50 Minutes**

½ box yellow cake mix with pudding (about 1⅔ cups)

⅓ cup water

¼ cup sour cream

3 tablespoons butter, melted

1 egg

1¼ cups miniature semisweet chocolate chips

½ teaspoon vegetable oil

1 Heat oven to 350°F. Spray bottom and sides of 9- or 8-inch square pan with baking spray with flour.

2 In large bowl, beat cake mix, water, sour cream, butter and egg with electric mixer on low speed 30 seconds. Beat on medium speed 2 minutes, scraping bowl occasionally. Stir in ½ cup of the chocolate chips. Spread in pan.

3 Bake 9-inch pan 22 to 28 minutes, 8-inch pan 27 to 33 minutes, or until toothpick inserted in center comes out clean. Cool completely, about 1 hour.

4 In small microwavable bowl, microwave ½ cup of the chocolate chips and the oil uncovered on High 45 seconds, stirring every 15 seconds, until melted. Place in small resealable food-storage plastic bag; cut off tiny corner of bag. Squeeze bag to drizzle over top of cake. Sprinkle with remaining ¼ cup chocolate chips. Store loosely covered.

1 Serving: Calories 270; Total Fat 14g (Saturated Fat 8g, Trans Fat 0g); Cholesterol 35mg; Sodium 210mg; Total Carbohydrate 35g (Dietary Fiber 1g); Protein 2g **Exchanges:** ½ Starch, 2 Other Carbohydrate, 2½ Fat **Carbohydrate Choices:** 2

Easy Chocolate-Banana Snack Cake

18 servings | **PREP TIME: 10 Minutes** | **START TO FINISH: 1 Hour 45 Minutes**

1 box devil's food cake mix with pudding

1 container (5.3 oz) 100-calorie fat-free Greek vanilla yogurt

1 cup mashed ripe bananas (2 or 3 medium)

¼ cup vegetable oil

3 eggs

¾ cup plus 2 tablespoons miniature semisweet chocolate chips

1 Heat oven to 350°F. Spray bottom only of 13 × 9-inch pan with cooking spray.

2 In large bowl, stir cake mix, yogurt, bananas, oil and eggs with spoon until well blended. Add ¾ cup chocolate chips; mix to distribute evenly in batter. Spread in pan. Sprinkle evenly with 2 tablespoons chocolate chips.

3 Bake 30 to 34 minutes or until toothpick inserted in center comes out clean. Cool completely, about 1 hour.

1 Serving: Calories 190; Total Fat 7g (Saturated Fat 3g, Trans Fat 0g); Cholesterol 30mg; Sodium 210mg; Total Carbohydrate 28g (Dietary Fiber 1g); Protein 3g **Exchanges:** 1 Starch, 1 Other Carbohydrate, 1½ Fat **Carbohydrate Choices:** 2

Sweet Secret For the best flavor, use bananas that have lots of brown specks on the skin and are slightly soft.

Sweet Secret Freeze ripe bananas in their peels when they can't be used right away. Thaw each banana 30 to 60 seconds in the microwave before using it in recipes.

Gluten-Free Chocolate Snack Cake with Creamy Butterscotch Frosting

16 servings | PREP TIME: 15 Minutes | START TO FINISH: 1 Hour 50 Minutes

CAKE

- ¼ cup white rice flour
- ¼ cup tapioca flour
- ¼ cup potato starch flour
- 3 tablespoons sweet white sorghum flour
- ¼ cup unsweetened baking cocoa
- 1 teaspoon xanthan gum
- 2 teaspoons gluten-free baking powder
- ½ teaspoon salt
- ½ cup sunflower oil
- ⅔ cup almond butter
- ½ cup packed brown sugar
- ½ cup granulated sugar
- 2 eggs
- ½ cup water

FROSTING

- ½ cup packed dark brown sugar
- ¼ cup melted ghee
- 3 to 4 tablespoons almond milk
- ⅛ teaspoon salt
- 1 cup gluten-free powdered sugar
- 2 tablespoons sliced almonds
- 2 tablespoons miniature semisweet choco-late chips

1 Heat oven to 350°F. Spray bottom and sides of 8-inch square pan with cooking spray (without flour).

2 In small bowl, mix flours, cocoa, xanthan gum, baking powder and ½ teaspoon salt with whisk; set aside. In medium bowl, beat oil, almond butter, ½ cup brown sugar, the granulated sugar, eggs and water with electric mixer on medium speed until well blended. Gradually add flour mixture, beating until well blended. Pour batter into pan.

3 Bake 30 to 35 minutes or until cake springs back when touched lightly in center. Cool completely in pan on cooling rack, about 1 hour.

4 Meanwhile, in 2-quart saucepan, place ½ cup brown sugar, the ghee, 3 tablespoons of the milk and ⅛ teaspoon salt. Heat to boiling over medium heat about 3 to 4 minutes, stirring constantly. Remove from heat; beat in powdered sugar until frosting is smooth and spreadable. If frosting is too thick, stir in additional almond milk, 1 teaspoon at a time. Frost cake. Sprinkle almonds and chocolate chips over top.

1 Serving: Calories 330; Total Fat 18g (Saturated Fat 3.5g, Trans Fat 0g); Cholesterol 35mg; Sodium 210mg; Total Carbohydrate 38g (Dietary Fiber 1g); Protein 3g **Exchanges:** ½ Starch, 2 Other Carbohydrate, 3½ Fat **Carbohydrate Choices:** 2½

Sweet Secret Gluten-free ingredients, such as almond butter made from ground almonds, provide vitamin E and monounsaturated fat. Look for almond butter in the baking aisle of your grocery store.

Cooking Gluten Free? Always read labels to make sure each recipe ingredient is gluten free. Products and ingredient sources can change.

Slow-Cooker Zebra Cake

10 servings | PREP TIME: **30 Minutes** | START TO FINISH: **6 Hours 25 Minutes**

CAKE

4	cups Easy Scratch Cake Mix (page 7)
1¼	cups milk
½	cup butter, softened
2	teaspoons vanilla
4	egg whites
¼	cup unsweetened baking cocoa

TOPPING

Sweetened Whipped Cream (page 6), if desired

Chocolate shavings, if desired

1 Line bottom and sides of 4-quart slow cooker with 1 piece of cooking parchment paper; trim edges if needed. Spray with cooking spray.

2 In large bowl, beat cake mix, milk, butter, vanilla and egg whites on low speed 30 seconds or until light and fluffy, scraping bowl occasionally. Beat on medium speed 3 minutes. Divide batter in half. Stir cocoa into half the batter.

3 Pour ½ cup chocolate batter into bottom of slow cooker using back of spoon or spatula to cover the bottom. Top with ½ cup white batter, taking care to layer but not mix the batters. Repeat layers until all batter has been used.

4 Place folded, clean dish towel under cover of cooker. Cook on Low heat setting 3 hours 30 minutes to 3 hours 45 minutes, carefully rotating slow cooker's ceramic insert 180 degrees (leaving cover on) after every 45 minutes or until toothpick inserted in center comes out clean. Uncover and transfer ceramic insert from slow cooker to cooling rack. Let stand 10 minutes.

5 Using parchment paper, carefully lift cake out of ceramic insert and transfer to cooling rack. Cool completely, about 2 hours. Remove parchment paper.

6 Serve with whipped cream and chocolate shavings.

1 Serving: Calories 360; Total Fat 10g (Saturated Fat 6g, Trans Fat 0g); Cholesterol 25mg; Sodium 350mg; Total Carbohydrate 59g (Dietary Fiber 1g); Protein 6g **Exchanges:** 2 Starch, 2 Other Carbohydrate, 2 Fat **Carbohydrate Choices:** 4

Sweet Secret The center may have a slightly wet look to it when done, so be sure your doneness test is with a toothpick.

Sweet Secret If you like, you can substitute one box white cake mix with pudding for the Easy Scratch Cake Mix. Prepare cake as directed on box using egg whites and adding 2 teaspoons vanilla to the batter. Divide batter in half; stir cocoa into half the batter. Continue as directed.

Chocolate-Mint Swirl Cake

16 servings | **PREP TIME: 20 Minutes** | **START TO FINISH: 2 Hours 30 Minutes**

FILLING

- 6 oz cream cheese (from 8-oz package), softened
- ¼ cup granulated sugar
- 1 tablespoon all-purpose flour
- 1 egg
- ⅛ teaspoon peppermint extract
- 3 drops green food color

CAKE

- 1 box devil's food cake mix with pudding
- ⅓ cup all-purpose flour
- 1 cup water
- ½ cup butter or margarine, melted
- 2 eggs

CHOCOLATE-MINT GLAZE

- 2 tablespoons semisweet chocolate chips
- 1 teaspoon shortening
- 1 cup powdered sugar
- ¼ teaspoon peppermint extract
- 1 or 2 drops green food color
- 1 tablespoon corn syrup
- 3 to 4 teaspoons water

1 Heat oven to 325°F. Grease 12-cup fluted tube cake pan; lightly flour. In small bowl, beat cream cheese with electric mixer on high speed until smooth and fluffy. Beat in granulated sugar, 1 tablespoon flour, 1 egg, ⅛ teaspoon peppermint extract and 3 drops food color until smooth; set aside.

2 In large bowl, beat cake mix, ⅓ cup flour, 1 cup water, the butter and 2 eggs on low speed 30 seconds, then on medium speed 2 minutes. Pour into pan. Spoon cream cheese filling over batter.

3 Bake 44 to 52 minutes or until toothpick inserted in center comes out clean. Cool in pan 15 minutes. Turn pan upside down onto cooling rack or heatproof plate; remove pan. Cool completely, about 1 hour.

4 In 1-quart saucepan, heat chocolate chips and shortening over low heat, stirring frequently, until melted; set aside. In small bowl, mix powdered sugar, ¼ teaspoon peppermint extract, 1 or 2 drops food color, the corn syrup and enough of the 3 to 4 teaspoons water to make a thick glaze that can be easily drizzled.

5 Drizzle over cake. Immediately spoon melted chocolate over glaze in ½-inch-wide ring. Working quickly, pull toothpick through chocolate to make swirls. Refrigerate until serving time. Store loosely covered in refrigerator.

1 Serving: Calories 270; Total Fat 12g (Saturated Fat 7g, Trans Fat 0g); Cholesterol 65mg; Sodium 310mg; Total Carbohydrate 37g (Dietary Fiber 0g); Protein 3g **Exchanges:** 1 Starch, 1½ Other Carbohydrate, 2½ Fat **Carbohydrate Choices:** 2½

Simple Sparkle Sprinkling with coarsely chopped chocolate mint candies makes this already incredible cake even more decadent!

Chocolate Lover's Dream Cake

16 servings | **PREP TIME: 20 Minutes** | **START TO FINISH: 3 Hours 35 Minutes**

CAKE

- 1 box butter recipe chocolate cake mix with pudding
- ¾ cup chocolate milk
- ⅓ cup butter, melted
- 3 eggs
- 1 container (8 oz) sour cream
- 1 package (4-serving size) chocolate fudge instant pudding and pie filling mix
- 1 bag (12 oz) semisweet chocolate chips (2 cups)

GLAZE

- ¾ cup semisweet chocolate chips
- 3 tablespoons butter
- 3 tablespoons light corn syrup
- 1½ teaspoons water

1 Heat oven to 350°F. Grease 12-cup fluted tube cake pan with shortening; lightly flour.

2 In large bowl, mix cake mix, chocolate milk, butter, eggs, sour cream and dry pudding mix with spoon until well blended (batter will be very thick). Stir in chocolate chips. Spoon into pan.

3 Bake 56 to 64 minutes or until top springs back when touched lightly in center. Cool 10 minutes. Turn pan upside down onto cooling rack or heatproof serving plate; remove pan. Cool completely, about 2 hours.

4 In 1-quart saucepan, heat glaze ingredients over low heat, stirring frequently, until chocolate chips are melted and mixture is smooth. Drizzle over cake. Store loosely covered.

1 Serving: Calories 400; Total Fat 20g (Saturated Fat 12g, Trans Fat 0g); Cholesterol 65mg; Sodium 390mg; Total Carbohydrate 50g (Dietary Fiber 2g); Protein 4g **Exchanges:** 1 Starch, 2½ Other Carbohydrate, 4 Fat **Carbohydrate Choices:** 3

Sweet Secret You don't want to lose even a drop of this divine batter, so measure the volume of your fluted tube cake pan using water to make sure it holds 12 cups. If the pan is smaller than 12 cups, the batter will overflow during baking.

Sweet Secret For a milder chocolate flavor, use milk chocolate chips instead of semisweet.

Strawberry-Covered Chocolate Bundt Cake

12 servings | PREP TIME: 20 Minutes | START TO FINISH: 2 Hours 30 Minutes

CAKE

- 1 box devil's food cake mix with pudding
- 1 box (4-serving size) chocolate instant pudding and pie filling mix
- 1 cup sour cream
- ¾ cup vegetable oil
- ⅓ cup water
- 3 eggs
- 1 cup chopped bittersweet chocolate

FROSTING

- 2 tablespoons butter, softened
- 2 tablespoons strawberry preserves
- 1⅓ cups powdered sugar
- 2 tablespoons buttermilk

GARNISH

- Fresh strawberries, if desired

1 Heat oven to 325°F. Grease 10- or 12-cup fluted tube cake pan with shortening; lightly flour.

2 In large bowl, beat all cake ingredients except bittersweet chocolate with electric mixer on low speed 1 minute, scraping bowl constantly. Increase speed to medium; beat 2 minutes. Stir in bittersweet chocolate until well combined. Pour into pan.

3 Bake 45 to 55 minutes or until toothpick inserted in center comes out clean. Cool 15 minutes. Turn upside down onto cooling rack or heatproof serving plate; remove pan. Cool completely, about 1 hour. Place cake on serving plate.

4 In medium bowl, beat butter and strawberry preserves with electric mixer on medium speed until smooth. Add powdered sugar, and beat until smooth. Beat in buttermilk. Pour over cake. Garnish with strawberries.

1 Serving: Calories 500; Total Fat 28g (Saturated Fat 10g, Trans Fat 0g); Cholesterol 60mg; Sodium 470mg; Total Carbohydrate 56g (Dietary Fiber 3g); Protein 5g **Exchanges:** 1½ Starch, 2 Other Carbohydrate, 5½ Fat **Carbohydrate Choices:** 4

Sweet Secret Swap out the strawberry preserves for your favorite fruit preserves.

Sweet Secret This cake was photographed using a specialty fluted tube cake pan. Deeper pans may require an additional 2 to 7 minutes of bake time.

Genius Ways to Frost a Cake

Wake up your cakes with these clever ways to frost them! Here are two fun and easy ways to frost cakes. **Mirror Glaze** adds a unique smooth and shiny coating for cake. Check out our **Mirror Glaze Secrets** for making it on page 200. **Magic Glaze** (page 200) a is ridiculously easy way to frost cakes in a hurry.

Mirror Glaze

3 cups | **PREP TIME: 15 Minutes** | **START TO FINISH: 1 Hour 45 Minutes**

1½	cups white vanilla baking chips, chopped
2	envelopes unflavored gelatin
⅔	cup cold water
1	cup sugar
⅔	cup light corn syrup
½	cup (from 14-oz can) sweetened condensed milk (not evaporated)
1 to 2	drops gel food color

1 Place baking chips in medium bowl. Set aside. In small bowl, sprinkle gelatin on ⅓ cup of the water to soften.

2 In 2-quart saucepan, cook remaining ⅓ cup water, sugar and corn syrup over medium heat 5 to 6 minutes or until sugar is dissolved. Remove from heat. Stir in gelatin until dissolved. Stir in sweetened condensed milk until well blended. Pour hot sugar-gelatin mixture over baking chips; let stand 5 minutes. Stir until smooth. Cool to 30 minutes or until mixture is between 85°F to 90°F. Carefully stir in food color until well blended and desired color.

3 Starting at center of cold cake, slowly pour glaze evenly over cake allowing to run down sides to cover. Refrigerate 30 minutes to set. Transfer to serving platter.

2 Tablespoons: Calories 160; Total Fat 3.5g (Saturated Fat 2.5g, Trans Fat 0g); Cholesterol 0mg; Sodium 50mg; Total Carbohydrate 29g (Dietary Fiber 0g); Protein 1g **Exchanges:** 2 Other Carbohydrate, ½ Fat **Carbohydrate Choices:** 2

Mirror Glaze Secrets

You'll love these tips when making Mirror Glaze (page 198).

Sweet Secret Any remaining glaze can be covered and refrigerated up to 1 week to use on another cake. To reheat, place in medium microwaveable bowl, microwave uncovered on High 1 to 1½ minutes, stirring every 30 seconds until between 85°F and 90°F. If necessary, scoop up any glaze that has fallen on the parchment paper with a spoon to pour over cake to completely cover top and sides.

Sweet Secret If you like, use Mirror Glaze on top of plain cake (no crumb coating needed), but the cake must be cold for it to glaze properly, so refrigerate the cooled cake 30 minutes before glazing. Without the frosting, you can see through the glaze to the plain cake.

Simple Sparkle Garnish glazed cake with fresh berries before refrigerating to set glaze. Add fresh mint or lemon leaves before serving.

Magic Glaze

Did you know creamy ready-to-spread frosting can quickly be turned into a cake glaze?

1 Spoon about ½ cup creamy chocolate ready-to-spread frosting into a small microwavable bowl.

2 Microwave uncovered on High about 15 seconds or until frosting can be stirred smooth and is thin enough to drizzle. (Or spoon frosting into 1-quart saucepan and heat over low heat, stirring constantly, until thin enough to drizzle.)

3 Glazes top of one 12-cup bundt cake, 10-inch angel food cake, 13 x 9-inch cake or 8- or 9-inch layer cake.

Sweet Secret It doesn't take an entire can of frosting to glaze a cake, so spooning it into a bowl to heat will leave frosting you can use for another occasion!

Simple Sparkle Before the glaze has a chance to set on the cake, sprinkle with crushed hard candies, cookies or chopped nuts.

Simple Sparkle Heat vanilla frosting with the same technique and drizzle cake alternately with chocolate and vanilla frostings for zebra effect.

Silver White Cake with Mirror Glaze

12 servings | PREP TIME: 20 Minutes | TOTAL: 2 Hours 15 Minutes

CAKE

2 ¼	cups all-purpose flour
1 ⅔	cups sugar
⅔	cup shortening
1 ¼	cups milk
3 ½	teaspoons baking powder
1	teaspoon salt
1	teaspoon vanilla or almond extract
5	egg whites

CARDBOARD, FROSTING AND GLAZE

13 x 9	piece of cardboard, covered with foil
⅔	cup vanilla ready-to-spread frosting Mirror Glaze (page 198)

1 Heat oven to 350°F. Grease 13 × 9-inch pan with shortening; lightly flour. Line 15 × 10 × 1-inch pan with cooking parchment paper.

2 In large bowl, beat all ingredients except egg whites and frosting with electric mixer on low speed 30 seconds, scraping bowl constantly. Beat on high speed 2 minutes, scraping bowl occasionally. Beat in egg whites on high speed 2 minutes, scraping bowl occasionally. Pour batter into pan.

3 Bake 40 to 45 minutes, or until toothpick inserted in center comes out clean or until cake springs back when touched lightly in center. Cool 10 minutes; invert cake onto 13 × 9-inch cardboard. Place cake and cardboard on cooling rack. Cool completely, about 1 hour.

4 Place cooled cake on cardboard on cooling rack over parchment paper–lined pan. Frost top and sides of cake with thin layer of frosting. Refrigerate 30 minutes or until frosting is hardened. Keep refrigerated until ready to top with Mirror Glaze.

5 Frost top and sides of cake with Mirror Glaze.

1 Serving: Calories 320; Total Fat 12g (Saturated Fat 3g, Trans Fat 0g); Cholesterol 0mg; Sodium 370mg; Total Carbohydrate 47g (Dietary Fiber 0g); Protein 4g **Exchanges:** 1 Starch, 2 Other Carbohydrate, 2 ½ Fat **Carbohydrate Choices:** 3

Chocolate Chip Cake
Fold ½ cup miniature or finely chopped regular semisweet chocolate chips into batter after beating in egg whites.

Cookies 'n Creme Cake
Stir 1 cup crushed creme-filled chocolate sandwich cookies into batter after beating in egg whites. Bake and cool as directed. Frost with Fluffy White Frosting; garnish with whole or coarsely crushed creme-filled chocolate sandwich cookies.

Marble Cake
Reserve 1¾ cups of the batter. Pour remaining batter into pan(s). Stir 3 tablespoons unsweetened baking cocoa and ⅛ teaspoon baking soda into reserved batter. Drop chocolate batter by tablespoonfuls randomly onto white batter. Cut through batters with knife for marbled design. Bake as directed.

Chocolate Chip–Caramel Poke Cake

15 servings | **PREP TIME: 20 Minutes** | **START TO FINISH: 2 Hours 35 Minutes**

1 box devil's food cake mix with pudding

1¼ cups buttermilk

½ cup vegetable oil

3 eggs

2 cups semisweet chocolate chips (about 12 oz)

1 cup caramel topping

½ cup vanilla creamy ready-to-spread frosting

Simple Sparkle If you like, you can also drizzle a little extra caramel topping over the top of the cake for a chocolate-caramel duo.

1 Heat oven to 350°F. Spray bottom only of 13 × 9-inch pan with baking spray with flour.

2 In large bowl, beat cake mix, buttermilk, oil and eggs with electric mixer on low speed 30 seconds, then on medium speed 2 minutes, scraping bowl occasionally. Pour batter into pan. Sprinkle with chocolate chips; press gently into batter.

3 Bake 35 to 43 minutes or until toothpick inserted in center comes out clean. Cool 30 minutes. Spray long-tined fork with cooking spray; poke holes halfway down into cake every inch with fork. Pour caramel topping over cake; spread evenly over surface, working back and forth to fill holes. Cool completely on cooling rack, about 1 hour.

4 In medium microwavable bowl, microwave frosting uncovered on High 15 to 30 seconds; stir until very soft. Spoon frosting into 1-quart resealable food-storage plastic bag; seal bag. Cut small tip off one bottom corner of bag; squeeze bag to drizzle frosting across top of cake. Store covered at room temperature.

1 Serving: Calories 450; Total Fat 20g (Saturated Fat 7g, Trans Fat 1g); Cholesterol 45mg; Sodium 410mg; Total Carbohydrate 63g (Dietary Fiber 2g); Protein 5g **Exchanges:** 1 Starch, 3 Other Carbohydrate, 4 Fat **Carbohydrate Choices:** 4

Chocolate Pudding Poke Cake

12 servings | **PREP TIME: 10 Minutes** | **START TO FINISH: 3 Hours 50 Minutes**

1   box chocolate fudge cake mix with pudding

1¼ cups water

½   cup vegetable oil

3   eggs

1   box (4-serving size) chocolate instant pudding and pie filling mix

2   cups cold milk

Sweetened Whipped Cream (page 6), if desired

Toasted chopped walnuts, if desired

1 Heat oven to 350°F. Grease bottom only of 13 × 9-inch pan with shortening or cooking spray.

2 Make cake mix as directed on box, using water, oil and eggs. Pour into pan. Bake and cool as directed on box for 13 × 9-inch pan.

3 With handle of wooden spoon (¼ to ½ inch diameter), poke holes halfway down into cake every ½ inch. In medium bowl, beat pudding mix and milk with whisk about 2 minutes. Pour pudding evenly over cake. Run knife around sides of pan to loosen cake. Cover and refrigerate about 2 hours or until chilled. Spread whipped cream over cake; sprinkle with walnuts. Store loosely covered in refrigerator.

1 Serving: Calories 290; Total Fat 13g (Saturated Fat 3g, Trans Fat 0g); Cholesterol 55mg; Sodium 470mg; Total Carbohydrate 38g (Dietary Fiber 1g); Protein 4g **Exchanges:** 1 Starch, 1½ Other Carbohydrate, 2½ Fat **Carbohydrate Choices:** 2½

Sweet Secret You can use chocolate fudge instead of chocolate pudding.

Sweet Secret To toast walnuts, sprinkle in ungreased heavy skillet. Cook over medium heat 5 to 7 minutes, stirring frequently until walnuts begin to brown, then stirring constantly until walnuts are light brown.

Simple Sparkle Instead of topping the cake with whipped topping and nuts, try serving with a scoop of fudge swirl ice cream.

Chocolate Molten Lava Mug Cake Mix

Makes 20 mug cakes | **PREP TIME: 15 Minutes** | **START TO FINISH: 15 Minutes**

1   box dark chocolate cake mix with pudding

1⅓   cups white angel food cake mix (½ box)

Water

4   bars (4.25 oz each) mildly sweet chocolate

Whipped topping, if desired

1 In gallon-size resealable food-storage plastic bag, combine cake mixes; seal bag and shake well to mix.

2 To make 1 mug cake, spray microwavable mug (about 12 oz) with cooking spray. Place 3 tablespoons dry cake mixture into mug. Add 2 tablespoons water; stir well to blend. Place 3 chocolate bar rectangles (not overlapping) on top of cake batter in mug.

3 Microwave uncovered on High 45 seconds to 1 minute or until cake is slightly moist on top. Do not overcook or cake will be dry. Let stand 1 minute. Turn upside down onto serving plate, or serve in mug. Top with whipped topping.

1 Mug Cake: Calories 250; Total Fat 8g (Saturated Fat 5g, Trans Fat 0g); Cholesterol 0mg; Sodium 290mg; Total Carbohydrate 42g (Dietary Fiber 2g); Protein 3g **Exchanges:** 1 Starch, 2 Other Carbohydrate, 1½ Fat **Carbohydrate Choices:** 3

Sweet Secret You can use 2 tablespoons chocolate chips or 2 miniature candy bars in place of the chocolate bar rectangles for each mug. For more gooey goodness, add 1 tablespoon marshmallows after cooking, and microwave 5 to 10 seconds longer.

Sweet Secret Try another flavor cake mix to add to the other half of the angel food cake mix.

Chocolate-Hazelnut Pudding Cake

9 servings | PREP TIME: 20 Minutes | START TO FINISH: 1 Hour 25 Minutes

CAKE

- 1 cup all-purpose flour
- ¾ cup granulated sugar
- ⅓ cup (2 oz) hazelnuts (filberts), ground
- 2 tablespoons unsweetened baking cocoa
- 2 teaspoons baking powder
- ½ cup milk
- ¼ cup hazelnut-flavored liqueur or coffee syrup
- 2 tablespoons vegetable oil
- 1 cup packed brown sugar
- ¼ cup unsweetened baking cocoa
- 1¾ cups boiling water

HAZELNUT WHIPPED CREAM

- ¾ cup whipping cream
- 1 tablespoon powdered sugar
- 1 tablespoon hazelnut-flavored liqueur

1 Heat oven to 350°F. Grease 8-inch square (2-quart) glass baking dish with cooking spray or shortening.

2 In medium bowl, stir together flour, granulated sugar, hazelnuts, 2 tablespoons cocoa and the baking powder. Stir in milk, ¼ cup liqueur and the oil. Spread batter in pan. Sprinkle with brown sugar and ¼ cup cocoa. Pour boiling water over top.

3 Bake 40 to 45 minutes or until center is set. Cool 20 minutes.

4 Meanwhile, in chilled small bowl, beat whipping cream with electric mixer on high speed, gradually adding powdered sugar and 1 tablespoon liqueur, until stiff peaks form. (Do not overbeat.)

5 Spoon warm pudding cake into dessert bowls. Spoon pudding over cake. Top with whipped cream.

1 Serving: Calories 350; Total Fat 11g (Saturated Fat 5g, Trans Fat 0g); Cholesterol 25mg; Sodium 130mg; Total Carbohydrate 60g (Dietary Fiber 1g); Protein 3g **Exchanges:** 1 Starch, 3 Other Carbohydrate, 2 Fat **Carbohydrate Choices:** 4

Sweet Secret Use a mini food processor to grind the hazelnuts.

Simple Sparkle Add whole hazelnuts to each serving of cake.

Chocolate-Hazelnut Lava Cakes

12 servings | **PREP TIME: 10 Minutes** | **START TO FINISH: 20 Minutes**

1   teaspoon shortening

1   tablespoon all-purpose flour

⅓   cup semisweet chocolate chips

1   tablespoon vegetable oil

1   cup powdered sugar

¾   cup fat-free egg product

⅓   cup hazelnut spread with cocoa

½   cup all-purpose flour

2   tablespoons powdered sugar

1 Heat oven to 400°F. Lightly grease 12 regular-size muffin cups with shortening and lightly flour.

2 In medium bowl, combine chocolate chips and oil. Microwave uncovered on High 1 to 2 minutes, stirring every 30 seconds, until chocolate is melted and smooth. Stir in 1 cup powdered sugar and the egg product with whisk until blended. Stir in hazelnut spread and flour. Divide batter evenly among muffin cups, filling each about three-fourths full.

3 Bake 9 minutes or until sides are firm (centers will be soft). Let stand 1 minute. Place serving platter upside down over muffin cups. Turn platter and muffin cups over; remove muffin cups. Sprinkle cakes with 2 tablespoons powdered sugar; serve warm.

1 Serving: Calories 160; Total Fat 5g (Saturated Fat 1.5g, Trans Fat 0g); Cholesterol 0mg; Sodium 35mg; Total Carbohydrate 24g (Dietary Fiber 1g); Protein 2g **Exchanges:** ½ Starch, 1 Other Carbohydrate, 1 Fat **Carbohydrate Choices:** 1½

Simple Sparkle Serve this delicious cake with fresh berries for a delightful taste combination.

Healthified Chocolate-Almond Pudding Cake

9 servings | **PREP TIME: 20 Minutes** | **START TO FINISH: 1 Hour 30 Minutes**

1   cup all-purpose flour

½   cup granulated sugar

¼   cup chopped almonds, toasted

¼   cup unsweetened baking cocoa

2   teaspoons baking powder

¼   teaspoon salt

½   cup fat-free (skim) milk

2   tablespoons vegetable oil

2   teaspoons vanilla

¼   teaspoon almond extract

¾   cup packed brown sugar

¼   cup unsweetened baking cocoa

1¾   cups water

       Vanilla reduced-fat ice cream, if desired

1 Heat oven to 350°F. Spray 8-inch square (2-quart) glass baking dish with cooking spray.

2 In medium bowl, mix flour, granulated sugar, almonds, ¼ cup cocoa, the baking powder and salt. Stir in milk, oil, vanilla and almond extract until blended. Spread batter in pan.

3 In 1-quart saucepan, mix brown sugar and ¼ cup cocoa with whisk. Stir in water; heat just to boiling, stirring occasionally. Pour over batter.

4 Bake 35 to 40 minutes or until center is set. Cool 30 minutes.

5 Spoon warm cake into individual dessert bowls. Spoon pudding from baking dish over cake. Serve with ice cream.

1 Serving: Calories 240; Total Fat 6g (Saturated Fat 1g, Trans Fat 0g); Cholesterol 0mg; Sodium 190mg; Total Carbohydrate 44g (Dietary Fiber 2g); Protein 3g **Exchanges:** 1 Starch, 2 Other Carbohydrate, 1 Fat **Carbohydrate Choices:** 3

Sweet Secret To toast almonds, heat oven to 350°F. Spread almonds in ungreased shallow pan. Bake uncovered 6 to 10 minutes, stirring occasionally, until light brown.

Sweet Secret For a mocha-flavored dessert, add 2 teaspoons instant coffee granules to the batter mixture.

Hot Fudge Sundae Cake

9 servings | **PREP TIME: 20 Minutes** | **START TO FINISH: 1 Hour 15 Minutes**

1	cup all-purpose flour
¾	cup granulated sugar
2	tablespoons baking cocoa
2	teaspoons baking powder
¼	teaspoon salt
½	cup milk
2	tablespoons vegetable oil
1	teaspoon vanilla
1	cup chopped nuts, if desired
1	cup packed brown sugar
¼	cup baking cocoa
1¾	cups very hot water
	Ice cream, if desired

1 Heat oven to 350ºF. In ungreased 9-inch square pan, mix flour, granulated sugar, 2 tablespoons cocoa, the baking powder and salt. Mix in milk, oil and vanilla with fork until smooth. Stir in nuts. Spread in pan.

2 Sprinkle brown sugar and ¼ cup cocoa over batter. Pour water over batter. Bake about 40 minutes or until top is dry. Cool 15 minutes.

3 Spoon warm cake into dessert dishes. Top with ice cream. Spoon sauce from pan over each serving.

1 Serving: Calories 255; Total Fat 4g (Saturated Fat 1g, Trans Fat 0g); Cholesterol 0mg; Sodium 190mg; Total Carbohydrate 54g (Dietary Fiber 2g); Protein 3g **Exchanges:** 1 Starch, 2 Fruit, 1 Fat **Carbohydrate Choices:** 3½

Sweet Secret
Have an ice-scream! Serve up this fun dessert at your next get-together, and include other ice-cream toppings such as chopped nuts, crushed cookies, candy sprinkles and maraschino cherries.

Chocolate Malt Ice-Cream Cake

16 servings | **PREP TIME: 30 Minutes** | **START TO FINISH: 7 Hours 5 Minutes**

1½ cups all-purpose flour

1 cup sugar

¼ cup unsweetened baking cocoa

1 teaspoon baking soda

½ teaspoon salt

⅓ cup vegetable oil

1 teaspoon white vinegar

1 teaspoon vanilla

1 cup water

1¼ cups chocolate fudge topping

1½ quarts (6 cups) vanilla ice cream, slightly softened

2 cups malted milk ball candies, coarsely chopped

1 cup whipping cream

Additional malted milk ball candies, if desired

1 Heat oven to 350°F. Grease bottom and side of 9- or 10-inch springform pan with shortening; lightly flour.

2 In large bowl, stir together flour, sugar, cocoa, baking soda and salt. Add oil, vinegar, vanilla and water; stir vigorously about 1 minute or until well blended. Immediately pour into pan.

3 Bake 30 to 35 minutes or until toothpick inserted in center comes out clean. Cool completely, about 1 hour.

4 Spread 1 cup of the fudge topping over cake. Freeze about 1 hour or until topping is firm.

5 In a large bowl, mix ice cream and coarsely chopped candies; spread over cake. Freeze about 4 hours or until ice cream is firm.

6 In chilled medium bowl, beat whipping cream with electric mixer on high speed until stiff peaks form. Remove side of pan; place cake on serving plate. Top with whipped cream. Melt remaining ¼ cup fudge topping; drizzle over whipped cream. Garnish with additional candies. Store covered in the freezer no longer than 1 week.

1 Serving: Calories 440; Total Fat 19g (Saturated Fat 10g, Trans Fat 0.5g); Cholesterol 40mg; Sodium 260mg; Total Carbohydrate 63g (Dietary Fiber 1g); Protein 4g **Exchanges:** 1½ Starch, 2½ Other Carbohydrate, 3½ Fat **Carbohydrate Choices:** 4

Creepy Ice-Cream and Cookies Cake

24 servings | **PREP TIME: 25 Minutes** | **START TO FINISH: 3 Hours 55 Minutes**

½   gallon (8 cups) cookies 'n cream ice cream, softened

1   box devil's food cake mix with pudding

1¼   cups water

½   cup vegetable oil

3   eggs

1   box (6-serving size) chocolate instant pudding and pie filling mix

2   cups milk

20   creme-filled chocolate sandwich cookies, crushed

1   package (8.4 oz) gummy worm candies

1 Line 13 x 9-inch pan with waxed paper, leaving about 2 inches of waxed paper overhanging all sides of pan. Press ice cream evenly in pan. Cover with plastic wrap; freeze 2 hours or until firm.

2 Heat oven to 350°F. Grease bottom only of another 13 x 9-inch pan with shortening or cooking spray; line pan with cooking parchment paper.

3 Make and bake cake mix as directed on box, using water, oil and eggs. Cool 10 minutes; run knife around side of pan to loosen. Place cooling rack upside down over pan; turn rack and pan over. Remove pan and paper. Cool cake completely, about 1 hour.

4 Meanwhile, in medium bowl, beat pudding mix and milk with wire whisk 2 minutes; let stand 3 minutes. Cover; refrigerate 1 hour.

5 Split cake horizontally to make 2 layers. Return bottom layer of cake to pan. Use waxed paper to lift ice cream from pan. Place ice cream on top of cake layer; top with remaining cake layer. Spread pudding evenly on cake. Sprinkle with cookie crumbs and gummy worm candies. Serve immediately. Store covered in freezer.

1 Serving: Calories 360; Total Fat 16g (Saturated Fat 6g, Trans Fat 0g); Cholesterol 0mg; Sodium 313mg; Total Carbohydrate 52g (Dietary Fiber 1g); Protein 5g **Exchanges:** 3 Other Carbohydrate, ½ Milk, 2 Fat **Carbohydrate Choices:** 3 ½

Simple Sparkle To create "tombstones" use 2 or 3 oval creme-filled or peanut-shaped peanut butter-filled sandwich cookies and cut each in half crosswise. Arrange cookies, cut side down, in the crushed cookies. Decorate if desired.

Sweet Secret Use your favorite flavor of ice cream in place of the cookies 'n cream ice cream.

Raspberry–White Chocolate Heart Cakes

16 cupcakes | PREP TIME: 30 Minutes | START TO FINISH: 2 Hours

RASPBERRY PUREE

¾ cup fresh or frozen raspberries, thawed

CUPCAKES

2 oz white chocolate baking bars (from 6-oz package)

¼ cup vegetable oil

½ cup sour cream

3 egg whites

1 teaspoon vanilla

2 cups Easy Scratch Cake Mix (page 7)

FROSTING

¾ cup whipped vanilla ready-to-spread frosting

1 Heat oven to 350°F. Place paper baking cup in each of 16 regular-size muffin cups; spray with cooking spray. Cut eight 12 × 2-inch strips of foil; cut each strip in half. Roll each piece of foil into a ball, about ¾ inch in diameter; set aside.

2 In small bowl, mash raspberries with fork; set aside. In large microwavable bowl, microwave white chocolate and oil on High 1 to 2 minutes, stirring every 30 seconds, until mixture can be stirred smooth. Add sour cream, egg whites and vanilla. Beat on medium speed with electric mixer 1 minute, scraping bowl occasionally, or until fluffy. On low speed, gradually beat in cake mix, scraping bowl occasionally, until dry ingredients are moistened.

3 Divide batter evenly among muffin cups. Spoon about ½ teaspoon raspberry puree onto center of each cupcake (reserve remaining puree for frosting). Place foil ball between cupcake liner and edge of cup to form heart shape.

4 Bake 20 to 25 minutes or until toothpick inserted in center comes out clean. Cool 5 minutes; remove from pan to cooling rack. Cool completely, about 1 hour.

5 In medium bowl, stir reserved raspberry puree into frosting just until mixed. Spread frosting over cupcakes.

1 Cupcake: Calories 190; Total Fat 8g (Saturated Fat 3.5g, Trans Fat 0g); Cholesterol 0mg; Sodium 105mg; Total Carbohydrate 26g (Dietary Fiber 0g); Protein 2g **Exchanges:** 1 Starch, ½ Other Carbohydrate, 1½ Fat **Carbohydrate Choices:** 2

Sweet Secret No raspberries? Try with fresh or frozen strawberries.

Simple Sparkle Treat your loved ones to these heart-shaped cupcakes on Valentine's Day, Mother's Day or anytime you want someone to feel special.

Chocolate Cupcakes with Salted Caramel Buttercream

24 cupcakes | **PREP TIME: 45 Minutes** | **START TO FINISH: 1 Hour 10 Minutes**

CUPCAKES

2	cups all-purpose flour
⅔	cup unsweetened baking cocoa
1	teaspoon baking soda
½	teaspoon baking powder
¼	teaspoon salt
⅔	cup butter, softened
1⅓	cups granulated sugar
2	eggs
1½	teaspoons vanilla
1	cup buttermilk

FROSTING

1½	cups butter, softened
4	cups powdered sugar
½	cup salted caramel sauce
2	tablespoons milk
1	teaspoon vanilla

GARNISH

2	tablespoons salted caramel sauce, slightly warmed
½	teaspoon coarse sea salt

1 Heat oven to 350°F. Place paper baking cup in each of 24 regular-size muffin cups. In medium bowl, mix flour, cocoa, baking soda, baking powder and ¼ teaspoon salt; set aside.

2 In large bowl, beat ⅔ cup softened butter and the granulated sugar with electric mixer on medium speed about 1 minute or until fluffy, scraping bowl occasionally. Beat in eggs, one at a time, until smooth. Stir in 1½ teaspoons vanilla. On low speed, gradually beat flour mixture into sugar mixture alternately with buttermilk, beating after each addition, just until smooth. Scrape side of bowl occasionally. Spoon batter evenly into muffin cups, filling each about two-thirds full.

3 Bake 18 to 22 minutes or until toothpick inserted in center comes out clean. Cool 10 minutes. Remove cupcakes from pan to cooling rack. Cool completely, about 30 minutes.

4 In large bowl, beat frosting ingredients with electric mixer on medium speed until smooth and spreadable. Frost cupcakes. Drizzle tops with 2 tablespoons caramel sauce; sprinkle with sea salt.

1 Cupcake: Calories 339; Total Fat 17.5g (Saturated Fat 11g, Trans Fat 0.5g); Cholesterol 60mg; Sodium 183mg; Total Carbohydrate 46g (Dietary Fiber 1g); Protein 3g **Exchanges:** 1 Starch, 2 Other Carbohydrate, 3½ Fat **Carbohydrate Choices:** 3

Sweet Secret You can pipe the frosting onto the cupcakes using a pastry bag and tip. Or you can fill a large resealable plastic bag with frosting; seal bag. Cut tip off one bottom corner, and squeeze bag to frost cupcakes.

Sweet Secret If you have only one pan and a recipe calls for more cupcakes than your pan will make, cover and refrigerate the rest of the batter while baking the first batch. Cool the pan about 15 minutes, then bake the rest of the batter, adding 1 to 2 minutes to the bake time.

Chocolate Marshmallow Creme–Filled Cupcakes

24 cupcakes | PREP TIME: 30 Minutes | START TO FINISH: 1 Hour 10 Minutes

CUPCAKES

1	box chocolate fudge cake mix with pudding
1¼	cups water
½	cup vegetable oil
3	eggs
¾	cup fluffy white whipped ready-to-spread frosting
¾	cup marshmallow creme

TOPPING

1	container rainbow chip creamy ready-to-spread frosting
¾	cup fluffy white whipped ready-to-spread frosting

1 Heat oven to 375°F. Place paper baking cup in each of 24 regular-size muffin cups. Make and bake cake mix as directed on box using water, oil and eggs. Cool 10 minutes; remove from pan to cooling racks. Cool completely, about 30 minutes.

2 Using melon baller or spoon, scoop out center of each cupcake, about 1 inch deep.

3 In small bowl, mix ¾ cup fluffy white frosting and ¾ cup marshmallow creme. Spoon frosting into corner of resealable heavy-duty food-storage plastic bag; seal bag. Cut small tip off one bottom corner of bag. Gently squeeze about 1 tablespoon frosting into center of each cupcake for filling.

4 In small bowl, mix topping ingredients. Spread over cupcakes. Store loosely covered.

1 Cupcake: Calories 260; Total Fat 11g (Saturated Fat 3g, Trans Fat 1.5g); Cholesterol 25mg; Sodium 220mg; Total Carbohydrate 37g (Dietary Fiber 0g); Protein 1g **Exchanges:** ½ Starch, 2 Other Carbohydrate, 2 Fat **Carbohydrate Choices:** 2½

Sweet Secret You can use other flavors of cake mix, too. Try strawberry, rainbow chip or lemon.

Simple Sparkle For a more festive look, add colorful sprinkles to the marshmallow creme filling.

Chocolate Extreme Cupcakes

12 cupcakes | PREP TIME: 25 Minutes | START TO FINISH: 1 Hour 45 Minutes

CUPCAKES

- 2 cups all-purpose flour
- 1 teaspoon baking soda
- ½ teaspoon salt
- 3 oz unsweetened baking chocolate, chopped
- 3 oz semisweet baking chocolate, chopped
- 1 cup butter, softened
- 1 cup packed brown sugar
- ½ cup granulated sugar
- 4 eggs
- 1 teaspoon vanilla
- 1 cup buttermilk

FROSTING

- 1 cup semisweet chocolate chips (6 oz)
- ½ cup butter, softened
- 4 cups powdered sugar
- ½ cup whipping cream
- 2 teaspoons vanilla
- Dash salt

1 Heat oven to 350°F. Place jumbo paper baking cup in each of 12 jumbo muffin cups.

2 In small bowl, mix flour, baking soda and ½ teaspoon salt; set aside. In small microwavable bowl, microwave unsweetened and semisweet baking chocolate uncovered on High 1 to 2 minutes, stirring once, until softened and chocolate can be stirred smooth.

3 In large bowl, beat 1 cup butter with electric mixer on medium speed until creamy. Gradually add brown sugar and granulated sugar, beating until well mixed. Add eggs, one at a time, beating well after each addition. Beat in melted chocolate and 1 teaspoon vanilla. On low speed, gradually beat in flour mixture alternately with buttermilk, beating just until blended. Divide batter evenly among muffin cups, filling each about three-fourths full.

4 Bake 30 minutes or until toothpick inserted in center comes out clean. Cool 5 minutes; remove from pans to cooling racks. Cool completely, about 45 minutes.

5 In small microwavable bowl, microwave chocolate chips uncovered on High 1 to 2 minutes, stirring once, until softened and chips can be stirred smooth. In large bowl, beat ½ cup butter with electric mixer on medium speed until creamy. On low speed, gradually beat in powdered sugar alternately with melted chocolate and whipping cream, beating until blended. Stir in 2 teaspoons vanilla and dash salt. Frost cupcakes.

1 Cupcake: Calories 753; Total Fat 40g (Saturated Fat 25g, Trans Fat 0g); Cholesterol 0mg; Sodium 164mg; Total Carbohydrate 99g (Dietary Fiber 3g); Protein 8g **Exchanges:** 1 Starch, 5½ Other Carbohydrate, ½ High-Fat Meat, 7 Fat **Carbohydrate Choices:** 6½

Vegan Chocolate-Avocado Cupcakes

12 cupcakes | **PREP TIME: 25 Minutes** | **START TO FINISH: 1 Hour 45 Minutes**

CUPCAKES

- 1½ cups all-purpose flour
- ⅓ cup unsweetened cocoa powder, sifted
- 1 cup vegan sugar
- 1 teaspoon ground cinnamon
- 1 teaspoon baking soda
- 1 teaspoon baking powder
- ¼ teaspoon salt
- 1 cup chocolate almond milk
- 1 tablespoon cider vinegar
- 1 large ripe avocado, pitted, peeled
- ¼ cup coconut oil, melted
- 1½ teaspoons vanilla

FROSTING

- ½ cup vegan sugar
- ¼ cup coconut oil
- 1 large ripe avocado, pitted, peeled
- ⅓ cup unsweetened cocoa powder, sifted
- 2 teaspoons vanilla
- ¼ teaspoon salt
- 2 tablespoons water

1 Heat oven to 350°F. Place paper baking cup in each of 12 regular-size muffin cups.

2 In large bowl, beat flour, cocoa powder, sugar, cinnamon, baking soda, baking powder and salt with whisk. In medium bowl, mix milk and vinegar; let stand 5 minutes. In food processor or blender, place 1 avocado, the milk mixture, coconut oil and vanilla. Cover; process until smooth, scraping bowl several times. Stir avocado mixture into flour mixture; mix well until smooth. Divide muffin batter evenly among muffin cups (cups will be full).

3 Bake 25 to 30 minutes or until toothpick inserted in center comes out clean. Cool 5 minutes; remove from pan to cooling rack. Cool completely, about 45 minutes.

4 Meanwhile, in microwavable bowl, heat sugar and coconut oil uncovered on High until oil has melted and sugar has softened, about 1 minute. In food processor or blender, place sugar mixture and remaining frosting ingredients. Cover; process 1 to 2 minutes, stopping to scrape down sides once or twice, until frosting is smooth. If too thick, add water, a teaspoon at a time, until desired consistency.

5 Frost cupcakes *immediately* or refrigerate frosting until ready to serve. Stir until spreading consistency and frost cupcakes.

1 Cupcake: Calories 310; Total Fat 14g (Saturated Fat 9g, Trans Fat 0g); Cholesterol 0mg; Sodium 260mg; Total Carbohydrate 44g (Dietary Fiber 4g); Protein 3g **Exchanges:** 1 Starch, 2 Other Carbohydrate, 2½ Fat **Carbohydrate Choices:** 3

Sweet Secret To quicken the ripening process of avocados, place them in a brown paper bag, and store at room temperature. For even faster ripening, add an apple to the bag.

Sweet Secret Always read labels to make sure each recipe ingredient is vegan. If you're unsure about any ingredient or product, check with the manufacturer.

Mini Chocolate Cupcakes Flag

80 cupcakes | **PREP TIME: 45 Minutes** | **START TO FINISH: 1 Hour 35 Minutes**

CUPCAKES

- 1 box devil's food cake mix with pudding
- 1¼ cups water
- 3 eggs
- 1 pouch (4 oz) 100% spinach puree

TOPPINGS

- 1½ cups Sweetened Whipped Cream (page 6)
- 1½ cups sliced small strawberries
- ½ cup fresh blueberries

1 Heat oven to 350°F. Place paper baking cup in each of 80 miniature muffin cups.

2 In large bowl, beat cupcake ingredients with electric mixer on low speed 30 seconds, then on medium speed 2 minutes, scraping bowl occasionally. Divide batter evenly among muffin cups, filling each about three-fourths full.

3 Bake 10 to 12 minutes or until toothpick inserted in center comes out clean. Cool 5 minutes; remove from pans to cooling racks. Cool completely, about 30 minutes.

4 Spread about 1 teaspoon whipped cream onto each cupcake. Arrange 70 cupcakes on tray as shown in photo. Place strawberries and blueberries on cupcakes to make stars-and-stripes pattern as shown in photo. Serve remaining cupcakes on another plate. Store in refrigerator.

1 Cupcake: Calories 35; Total Fat 1g (Saturated Fat 0.5g, Trans Fat 0g); Cholesterol 10mg; Sodium 50mg; Total Carbohydrate 5g (Dietary Fiber 0g); Protein 0g **Exchanges:** ½ Other Carbohydrate **Carbohydrate Choices:** ½

Sweet Secret Once decorated, these cupcakes will need to be stored in the refrigerator. But you can make these cute little cupcake gems another time and freeze them, unfrosted, to pull out for a special treat!

Sweet Secret You can substitute 1½ cups frozen whipped topping, thawed, for the Sweetened Whipped Cream.

CHAPTER FIVE

potpourri–
of–
flavors
cakes

Slow-Cooker Red Velvet Cake

12 servings | **PREP TIME: 15 Minutes** | **START TO FINISH: 3 Hours 10 Minutes**

1 box devil's food cake mix with pudding

1¼ cups water

½ cup vegetable oil

3 eggs

1 bottle (1 oz) red food color

1 container cream cheese creamy ready-to-spread frosting

1 Line bottom and sides of 5-quart slow cooker with 1 piece of cooking parchment paper; spray with cooking spray.

2 Make cake mix as directed on box, using water, oil and eggs and adding food color with the water. Pour batter into slow cooker.

3 Place folded, clean dish towel under cover of cooker. Cook on High heat setting 45 minutes. Leaving cover on, carefully rotate slow cooker's ceramic insert 180 degrees. Continue to cook on High heat setting 45 to 60 minutes or until toothpick inserted in center comes out clean. Uncover and transfer ceramic insert from slow cooker to cooling rack. Let stand 10 minutes.

4 Using parchment paper, carefully lift cake out of ceramic insert and transfer to cooling rack. Cool completely, about 1 hour. Remove parchment paper.

5 Spread frosting on cake.

1 Serving: Calories 380; Total Fat 17g (Saturated Fat 5g, Trans Fat 0g); Cholesterol 45mg; Sodium 390mg; Total Carbohydrate 54g (Dietary Fiber 0g); Protein 1g **Exchanges:** ½ Starch, 3 Other Carbohydrate, 3½ Fat **Carbohydrate Choices:** 3½

Sweet Secret Whipped fluffy white frosting makes a great substitute for the cream cheese frosting.

Simple Sparkle To make this cake sparkle, try sprinkling the top with red sugar.

Slow-Cooker Classic Coffee Cake

12 servings | **PREP TIME: 20 Minutes** | **START TO FINISH: 3 Hours 30 Minutes**

TOPPING

1	cup all-purpose flour
½	cup packed brown sugar
4	tablespoons butter, softened
2	teaspoons ground cinnamon
⅛	teaspoon salt

COFFEE CAKE

1	box yellow cake mix with pudding
1	cup sour cream
½	cup butter, melted
4	eggs

GLAZE

½	cup powdered sugar
2 to 3	teaspoons milk
¼	teaspoon vanilla

1 Line bottom and sides of 5-quart slow cooker with 1 sheet of cooking parchment paper; spray with cooking spray.

2 In medium bowl, stir topping ingredients until crumbly; set aside. In large bowl, stir cake ingredients until blended. Pour into slow cooker.

3 Place folded, clean dish towel under cover of cooker. Cook on High heat setting 1 hour. Carefully remove slow cooker's ceramic insert, and rotate insert 180 degrees. Sprinkle topping over cake. Replace cover with dish towel under the cover. Continue to cook on High heat setting 30 minutes to 1 hour or until toothpick inserted in center comes out clean. Transfer ceramic insert from slow cooker to cooling rack. Let stand 10 minutes.

4 Using parchment paper, carefully lift cake out of ceramic insert and transfer to cooling rack. Cool completely, about 1 hour. Remove parchment paper.

5 In small bowl, beat glaze ingredients until smooth. Drizzle over cake.

1 Serving: Calories 400; Total Fat 18g (Saturated Fat 11g, Trans Fat 0.5g); Cholesterol 105mg; Sodium 410mg; Total Carbohydrate 53g (Dietary Fiber 1g); Protein 4g **Exchanges:** 1 Starch, 2½ Other Carbohydrate, 3½ Fat **Carbohydrate Choices:** 3½

Sweet Secret If you like, add ½ cup chopped toasted walnuts or pecans to the topping mixture.

Simple Sparkle For an easier version, you can skip the glaze, and sprinkle powdered sugar on top of the cooled cake.

Slow-Cooker Citrus-Gingerbread Cake

12 servings | **PREP TIME: 20 Minutes** | **START TO FINISH: 4 Hours 30 Minutes**

1⅓ cups all-purpose flour

¾ cup packed brown sugar

1¼ teaspoons baking powder

¾ teaspoon ginger

½ teaspoon ground cinnamon

¼ teaspoon nutmeg

¼ teaspoon salt

¼ cup butter, melted

⅓ cup molasses

1 egg

½ cup milk

½ cup chopped dates

6 thin slices each orange and lemon

1 Line bottom and sides of 4-quart slow cooker with 1 piece of cooking parchment paper; trim edges if needed. Spray with cooking spray.

2 In medium bowl, combine flour, brown sugar, baking powder, ginger, cinnamon, nutmeg and salt until well blended. Mix in butter, molasses, egg and milk with whisk until well blended. Stir in dates. Spread batter evenly in slow cooker. Place orange and lemon slices around edge of cake, overlapping if needed, and tucking edges down along side of slow cooker.

3 Place folded, clean dish towel under cover of cooker. Cook on Low heat setting 3 hours to 3 hours 30 minutes, carefully rotating slow cooker's ceramic insert 180 degrees (leaving cover on) after every 45 minutes or until toothpick inserted in center comes out clean. Uncover and transfer ceramic insert from slow cooker to cooling rack. Let stand 10 minutes.

4 Using parchment paper, carefully lift cake out of ceramic insert and transfer to cooling rack. Cool 30 minutes. Remove parchment paper. Serve warm.

1 Serving: Calories 200; Total Fat 4.5g (Saturated Fat 2.5g, Trans Fat 0g); Cholesterol 25mg; Sodium 150mg; Total Carbohydrate 38g (Dietary Fiber 1g); Protein 2g **Exchanges:** ½ Starch, 2 Other Carbohydrate, 1 Fat **Carbohydrate Choices:** 2½

Sweet Secret Crumpling cooking parchment paper first and then placing inside the ceramic insert makes it easier to fit.

Sweet Secret Putting the citrus slices around the edges of the cake rather than in the center ensures that the middle of the cake will cook properly.

Simple Sparkle Sprinkle the citrus slices lightly with sugar after removing the insert from the slow cooker for a little sparkle and crunch.

Honey Bun Cake

12 servings | **PREP TIME: 15 Minutes** | **START TO FINISH: 2 Hours 5 Minutes**

CAKE

- 1 box yellow cake mix with pudding
- ⅔ cup vegetable oil
- 4 eggs
- 1 container (8 oz) sour cream (1 cup)
- 1 cup packed brown sugar
- ⅓ cup chopped pecans
- 2 teaspoons ground cinnamon

FROSTING

- 1 cup powdered sugar
- 1 tablespoon milk
- 1 teaspoon vanilla

1 Heat oven to 350°F. Grease and lightly flour 13 × 9-inch pan, or spray with baking spray with flour.

2 In large bowl, beat cake mix, oil, eggs and sour cream with electric mixer on low speed 30 seconds, then on medium speed 2 minutes, scraping bowl occasionally. Spread half of the batter in pan.

3 In small bowl, stir together brown sugar, pecans and cinnamon; sprinkle over batter in pan. Carefully spread remaining batter evenly over pecan mixture.

4 Bake 44 to 48 minutes or until deep golden brown. In another small bowl, stir powdered sugar, milk and vanilla until thin enough to spread. Prick surface of warm cake several times with fork. Spread powdered sugar mixture over cake. Cool completely, about 1 hour. Store covered.

1 Serving: Calories 440; Total Fat 21g (Saturated Fat 6g, Trans Fat 0g); Cholesterol 80mg; Sodium 300mg; Total Carbohydrate 60g (Dietary Fiber 1g); Protein 3g **Exchanges:** 1 Starch, 3 Other Carbohydrate, 4 Fat **Carbohydrate Choices:** 4

Gluten-Free Red Velvet Cake

12 servings | **PREP TIME: 15 Minutes** | **START TO FINISH: 1 Hour 55 Minutes**

1 box gluten-free devil's food cake mix

1 cup buttermilk

1 tablespoon gluten-free red food color

¼ teaspoon baking soda

½ cup butter, softened

3 eggs

1¼ cups cream cheese whipped ready-to-spread frosting

Unsweetened baking cocoa, if desired

1 Heat oven to 350°F. Generously spray bottom only of 8- or 9-inch square pan with cooking spray (without flour).

2 In large bowl, beat cake mix, buttermilk, food color, baking soda, butter and eggs with electric mixer on low speed 30 seconds, then on medium speed 2 minutes, scraping bowl occasionally. Pour batter into pan.

3 Bake 40 to 45 minutes or until toothpick inserted in center comes out clean. Cool on cooling rack 10 minutes. Run knife around sides of pan to loosen cake; remove from pan to cooling rack. Cool completely, about 45 minutes.

4 Place cake on serving plate. Frost top and sides of cake with cream cheese frosting; sprinkle with cocoa.

1 Serving: Calories 320; Total Fat 14g (Saturated Fat 7g, Trans Fat 1.5g); Cholesterol 75mg; Sodium 350mg; Total Carbohydrate 44g (Dietary Fiber 0g); Protein 3g **Exchanges:** 1 Starch, 2 Other Carbohydrate, 2½ Fat **Carbohydrate Choices:** 3

Sweet Secret For Gluten-Free Red Velvet Cupcakes, place a paper baking cup in each of 12 regular-size muffin cups. Make batter as directed in step 2 and divide evenly among muffin cups. Bake 18 to 23 minutes or until toothpick inserted in center comes out clean. Cool 5 minutes; remove from pan to cooling rack. Frost cooled cupcakes.

Cooking Gluten Free? Always read labels to make sure each recipe ingredient is gluten free. Products and ingredient sources can change.

Gluten-Free Cinnamon Roll Pound Cake with Vanilla Drizzle

8 servings | **PREP TIME: 25 Minutes** | **START TO FINISH: 2 Hours 30 Minutes**

CAKE

- 2 cups gluten-free all-purpose flour blend
- 2 teaspoons gluten-free baking powder
- ½ teaspoon salt
- 1 cup unsalted butter, softened
- ¾ cup granulated sugar
- 4 eggs
- 2½ teaspoons gluten-free vanilla
- 1 tablespoon ground cinnamon

VANILLA DRIZZLE

- ½ cup gluten-free powdered sugar
- 1 tablespoon milk

1. Heat oven to 350°F. Spray 9 × 5-inch loaf pan with cooking spray (without flour).

2. In small bowl, mix flour blend, baking powder and salt; set aside. In large bowl, beat butter and granulated sugar with electric mixer on medium-high speed until fluffy, about 3 minutes. Reduce speed to medium-low; gradually beat in eggs and 2 teaspoons of the vanilla until blended. Gradually add flour mixture, beating on low speed just until combined.

3. Transfer half of the batter to small bowl; stir in cinnamon. Alternately spoon plain batter and cinnamon batter into pan and swirl with knife.

4. Bake 40 to 50 minutes or until toothpick inserted in center comes out clean. Cool on cooling rack 15 minutes; remove from pan to cooling rack. Cool completely, about 1 hour.

5. In small bowl, mix powdered sugar, milk and remaining ½ teaspoon vanilla until smooth. Drizzle over cake.

1 Serving: Calories 480; Total Fat 26g (Saturated Fat 16g, Trans Fat 1g); Cholesterol 165mg; Sodium 480mg; Total Carbohydrate 54g (Dietary Fiber 2g); Protein 5g **Exchanges:** 1½ Starch, 2 Other Carbohydrate, 5 Fat **Carbohydrate Choices:** 3½

Sweet Secret Let the eggs stand at room temperature for 30 minutes before making this cake. If you forget to take them out of the refrigerator, just place them in a bowl and cover with warm water to take the chill off.

Cooking Gluten Free? Always read labels to make sure each recipe ingredient is gluten free. Products and ingredient sources can change.

Gluten-Free Layered Streusel Coffee Cake

9 servings | **PREP TIME: 20 Minutes** | **START TO FINISH: 1 Hour 25 Minutes**

STREUSEL

- ½ cup packed brown sugar
- ⅓ cup gluten-free all-purpose rice flour blend
- 1½ teaspoons ground cinnamon
- ¼ cup cold butter

COFFEE CAKE

- ¾ cup granulated sugar
- 6 tablespoons butter, softened
- 2 eggs
- ½ cup milk
- 1½ teaspoons gluten-free vanilla
- 1½ cups gluten-free all-purpose rice flour blend
- 2 teaspoons gluten-free baking powder
- ½ teaspoon salt

GLAZE

- ½ cup powdered sugar
- ¼ teaspoon gluten-free vanilla
- 2 to 3 teaspoons milk

1 Heat oven to 375°F. Spray bottom and sides of 8-inch square pan with cooking spray (without flour).

2 In medium bowl, mix brown sugar, ⅓ cup flour blend and the cinnamon. Cut in ¼ cup cold butter with pastry blender or fork until mixture is crumbly; set aside.

3 In large bowl, beat ¾ cup granulated sugar and the 6 tablespoons softened butter with electric mixer on medium speed until fluffy. Beat in eggs, one at a time, until blended. Beat in ½ cup milk and 1½ teaspoons vanilla just until blended. Stir in 1½ cups flour blend, the baking powder and salt. Spread half of batter in pan. Sprinkle about ¾ cup streusel mixture over batter. Drop remaining batter by spoonfuls over streusel; spread carefully. Sprinkle remaining streusel over batter.

4 Bake 30 to 35 minutes or until toothpick inserted in center of cake comes out clean. Cool at least 30 minutes.

5 In small bowl, mix glaze ingredients until smooth and thin enough to drizzle. Drizzle over warm coffee cake. Serve warm.

1 Serving: Calories 230; Total Fat 7g (Saturated Fat 4g, Trans Fat 0g); Cholesterol 55mg; Sodium 420mg; Total Carbohydrate 41g (Dietary Fiber 0g); Protein 2g **Exchanges:** ½ Starch, 2 Other Carbohydrate, 1½ Fat **Carbohydrate Choices:** 3

Sweet Secret You can make this coffee cake ahead of time and store covered at room temperature up to 2 days.

Cooking Gluten Free? Always read labels to make sure each recipe ingredient is gluten free. Products and ingredient sources can change.

Cinnamon Roll Coffee Cake

12 servings | **PREP TIME: 20 Minutes** | **START TO FINISH: 2 Hours 5 Minutes**

STREUSEL

½ cup packed brown sugar

½ cup chopped pecans

¼ cup butter, softened

1 tablespoon all-purpose flour

1 teaspoon ground cinnamon

CAKE

1 box doughnut-flavored cake mix with original doughnut glaze

⅔ cup water

⅓ cup vegetable oil

2 eggs

Ground cinnamon, if desired

1 Heat oven to 350°F. Grease 12-cup fluted tube cake pan with shortening; lightly flour.

2 In medium bowl, mix streusel ingredients with fork until well blended; set aside. In large bowl, mix cake mix (dry), water, oil and eggs with electric mixer on low speed 30 seconds, scraping bowl frequently. Beat on medium speed 2 minutes, scraping bowl occasionally. Pour about 1¼ cups batter into pan. Carefully spoon brown sugar mixture over batter, being sure the filling does not touch the edges. Pour remaining batter over filling.

3 Bake 30 to 35 minutes or until toothpick inserted in center comes out clean. Cool 10 minutes; remove from pan to serving plate. Squeeze pouch of glaze from cake mix 10 times. Cut ¼-inch top from corner of pouch. Drizzle glaze over warm cake. Sprinkle with cinnamon. Cool completely, about 1 hour.

1 Serving: Calories 320; Total Fat 16g (Saturated Fat 4.5g, Trans Fat 0g); Cholesterol 40mg; Sodium 200mg; Total Carbohydrate 42g (Dietary Fiber 0g); Protein 3g **Exchanges:** 1 Starch, 2 Other Carbohydrate, 3 Fat **Carbohydrate Choices:** 3

Sweet Secret We like pecans, but you can use chopped almonds, macadamia nuts or walnuts in the filling.

Sweet Secret You can substitute a box of white or yellow cake mix with pudding (and water, oil and eggs called for on the box) for the cake. Prepare the batter as directed on box. Pour 2 cups of the batter into pan. Sprinkle with streusel as directed in recipe; top with remaining cake batter. Bake as directed in step 3. Frost cake with your favorite glaze.

Almond Coffee Cake

9 servings | PREP TIME: 15 Minutes | START TO FINISH: 2 Hours

¾ cup butter, softened

1 cup granulated sugar

4 oz almond paste (⅓ cup)

½ teaspoon almond extract

2 eggs

1½ cups all-purpose flour

½ teaspoon baking powder

⅛ teaspoon salt

½ cup sliced almonds

Powdered sugar, if desired

1 Heat oven to 350°F. Line 8-inch square pan with foil, leaving 1 inch of foil overhanging at two opposite sides of pan. Spray foil with cooking spray.

2 In large bowl, beat butter, granulated sugar and almond paste with electric mixer on medium speed until light and fluffy. Beat in almond extract and eggs until well blended. On low speed, beat in flour, baking powder and salt just until blended. Spread batter in pan; sprinkle with almonds.

3 Bake 45 minutes or until toothpick inserted in center comes out clean. Cool completely in pan on cooling rack, about 1 hour. Use foil to lift cake out of pan. Sprinkle with powdered sugar.

1 Serving: Calories 410; Total Fat 22g (Saturated Fat 11g, Trans Fat 0.5g); Cholesterol 80mg; Sodium 210mg; Total Carbohydrate 47g (Dietary Fiber 2g); Protein 6g **Exchanges:** 2½ Starch, ½ Other Carbohydrate, 4 Fat **Carbohydrate Choices:** 3

Sweet Secret Look for almond paste in the bakery aisle at the grocery store. It's important to use fresh almond paste because if it is even slightly hardened, it will not mix well. Check the date on the package.

Simple Sparkle Garnish with fresh berries, raspberries, blackberries or blueberries for a colorful splash.

Whole Wheat Streusel Coffee Cake

12 servings | **PREP TIME: 15 Minutes** | **START TO FINISH: 1 Hour 50 Minutes**

STREUSEL

- ½ cup packed brown sugar
- 2 tablespoons whole wheat flour
- ⅓ cup chopped pecans, toasted
- ½ teaspoon ground cinnamon
- 1 tablespoon vegetable oil

COFFEE CAKE

- 1 cup all-purpose flour
- ½ cup whole wheat flour
- ¾ cup packed brown sugar
- 1 teaspoon baking powder
- ½ teaspoon baking soda
- ½ teaspoon salt
- 1 egg
- 1 egg white
- ¾ cup sour cream
- ¼ cup vegetable oil
- 1 teaspoon vanilla

1 Heat oven to 350°F. Spray bottom only of 9-inch square pan with cooking spray. In small bowl, mix streusel ingredients with fork until crumbly; set aside.

2 In large bowl, mix flours, ¾ cup brown sugar, the baking powder, baking soda and salt. Stir in remaining coffee cake ingredients until well blended.

3 Spoon half of batter into pan, spreading evenly. Sprinkle ½ cup of the streusel evenly over batter. Drop remaining batter by spoonfuls over streusel; carefully spread. Sprinkle with remaining streusel.

4 Bake 30 to 35 minutes or until toothpick inserted in center comes out clean. Cool about 1 hour. Serve warm.

1 Serving: Calories 201; Total Fat 8.2g (Saturated Fat 0.7g, Trans Fat 0g); Cholesterol 16.8mg; Sodium 215mg; Total Carbohydrate 29.6g (Dietary Fiber 1g); Protein 3.4g **Exchanges:** 1 Starch, 1½ Other Carbohydrate, 1½ Fat **Carbohydrate Choices:** 2½

Sweet Secret Toasting the pecans is a great way to add extra flavor. Heat oven to 350°F. Spread pecans in ungreased shallow pan. Bake uncovered 6 to 10 minutes, stirring occasionally, until light brown.

Sweet Secret If you like, you can use reduced-fat sour cream in this coffee cake.

Monkey Bread Coffee Cake

12 servings | **PREP TIME: 20 Minutes** | **START TO FINISH: 1 Hour 5 Minutes**

3 cups Original Bisquick mix

2 tablespoons granulated sugar

¼ cup butter, melted

¼ cup milk

1 teaspoon vanilla

3 eggs

¼ cup granulated sugar

½ teaspoon ground cinnamon

1 cup butter

¾ cup packed brown sugar

1 Heat oven to 350°F. Grease 12-cup fluted tube cake pan with shortening; lightly flour.

2 In large bowl, stir Bisquick mix, 2 tablespoons granulated sugar, ¼ cup butter, the milk, vanilla and eggs until soft dough forms. Divide dough into 24 pieces. With greased hands, roll dough into balls.

3 In small bowl, mix ¼ cup granulated sugar and the cinnamon. Roll each dough ball in sugar mixture; place balls randomly in pan. Sprinkle with any remaining sugar mixture.

4 In 2-quart saucepan, melt 1 cup butter over low heat. Stir in brown sugar. Heat to boiling over medium heat, stirring constantly. Boil 2 minutes; remove from heat. Pour caramel mixture over dough balls in pan.

5 Bake 22 to 28 minutes or until lightly browned on top. Cool 5 minutes. Place heatproof serving plate upside down over pan; carefully turn plate and pan over. Remove pan; immediately scrape any remaining topping in pan onto coffee cake. Serve warm.

1 Serving: Calories 380; Total Fat 22g (Saturated Fat 12g, Trans Fat 2g); Cholesterol 100mg; Sodium 510mg; Total Carbohydrate 40g (Dietary Fiber 0g); Protein 4g **Exchanges:** 2 Starch, ½ Other Carbohydrate, 4 Fat **Carbohydrate Choices:** 2½

Sweet Secret Be sure to firmly pack the brown sugar when measuring it for the caramel mixture.

Hummingbird Upside-Down Poke Bundt Cake

14 servings | **PREP TIME: 35 Minutes** | **START TO FINISH: 3 Hours 35 Minutes**

CAKE

- ½ cup plus 2 tablespoons butter, melted
- ⅓ cup packed brown sugar
- 6 pineapple slices (from 20-oz can), drained, juice reserved
- 1 box yellow cake mix with pudding
- ½ cup reserved pineapple juice
- 3 eggs
- 1 cup mashed very ripe bananas (2 medium)
- 1½ teaspoons ground cinnamon
- ½ teaspoon ground nutmeg

FILLING

- 1 cup (from 14-oz can) canned sweetened condensed milk (not evaporated)
- ¼ cup reserved pineapple juice

POWDERED SUGAR ICING

- ½ cup powdered sugar
- 2 teaspoons reserved pineapple juice
- 2 tablespoons chopped pecans, toasted

1 Heat oven to 350°F. Grease 12-cup fluted tube cake pan with shortening; lightly flour. Pour 2 tablespoons melted butter evenly in bottom of pan. Sprinkle brown sugar over butter. Cut pineapple slices in half. Line bottom of pan with pineapple halves, fitting slices close together. Set aside.

2 In large bowl, beat cake mix, ½ cup melted butter, ½ cup reserved pineapple juice, the eggs, bananas, cinnamon and nutmeg with electric mixer on medium speed 2 minutes. Pour over pineapple in pan.

3 Bake 40 to 45 minutes or until toothpick inserted in center comes out clean. Remove from oven; cool 15 minutes.

4 In small bowl, mix filling ingredients. With handle of wooden spoon (¼ to ½ inch in diameter), poke holes halfway down into cake every inch, wiping spoon handle occasionally to prevent sticking if necessary. Carefully pour filling evenly over surface, working back and forth to fill holes. Refrigerate, uncovered, about 2 hours or until chilled.

5 Remove from refrigerator. Run metal spatula around outer and inner sides of pan to loosen cake Turn upside down onto serving platter. In small bowl, mix powdered sugar and 2 teaspoons reserved pineapple juice. Drizzle on top of cake; sprinkle with pecans.

1 Serving: Calories 253; Total Fat 12.5g (Saturated Fat 7g, Trans Fat 0g); Cholesterol 71mg; Sodium 54mg; Total Carbohydrate 33g (Dietary Fiber 1g); Protein 4g **Exchanges:** 1½ Starch, 2 Other Carbohydrate, 2½ Fat **Carbohydrate Choices:** 3½

Sweet Secret To toast pecans, sprinkle in ungreased heavy skillet. Cook over medium-low heat 5 to 7 minutes, stirring frequently until browning begins, then stirring constantly until golden brown.

Pound Cake

24 servings | PREP TIME: 20 Minutes | START TO FINISH: 4 Hours

3 cups all-purpose flour

1 teaspoon baking powder

¼ teaspoon salt

2½ cups granulated sugar

1 cup butter, softened

1 teaspoon vanilla or almond extract

5 eggs

1 cup milk or evaporated milk

Powdered sugar, if desired

1 Heat oven to 350°F. Generously grease bottom, side and tube of 10-inch angel food (tube) cake pan, 12-cup fluted tube cake pan or 2 (9 × 5-inch) loaf pans with shortening; lightly flour.

2 In medium bowl, mix flour, baking powder and salt; set aside. In large bowl, beat granulated sugar, butter, vanilla and eggs with electric mixer on low speed 30 seconds, scraping bowl constantly. Beat on high speed 5 minutes, scraping bowl occasionally. Beat flour mixture into sugar mixture alternately with milk on low speed, beating just until smooth after each addition. Pour into pan(s).

3 Bake angel food or fluted tube cake pan 1 hour 10 minutes to 1 hour 20 minutes, loaf pans 55 to 60 minutes, or until toothpick inserted in center comes out clean. Cool 20 minutes; remove from pan(s) to cooling rack. Cool completely, about 2 hours. Sprinkle with powdered sugar.

1 Serving: Calories 230; Total Fat 9g (Saturated Fat 4.5g, Trans Fat 0g); Cholesterol 65mg; Sodium 115mg; Total Carbohydrate 33g (Dietary Fiber 0g); Protein 3g **Exchanges:** 1 Starch, 1 Other Carbohydrate, 2 Fat **Carbohydrate Choices:** 2

Sweet Secret For Cranberry-Orange Pound Cake, stir in ½ cup coarsely chopped fresh cranberries or dried cranberries and 1 teaspoon grated orange peel before pouring into pan. Bake as directed.

Neapolitan Cake

12 to 16 servings | **PREP TIME: 20 Minutes** | **START TO FINISH: 2 Hours 15 Minutes**

1 box white cake mix with pudding

1 cup water

¼ cup vegetable oil

3 egg whites

¼ teaspoon almond extract

10 drops red food color

¼ cup chocolate-flavor syrup

½ cup chocolate creamy ready-to-spread frosting

1 Heat oven to 325°F. Grease 12-cup fluted tube cake pan with shortening; lightly flour.

2 In large bowl, beat cake mix, water, oil and egg whites with electric mixer on low speed 30 seconds, then on medium speed 2 minutes, scraping bowl occasionally. Pour about 1⅔ cups batter into pan.

3 Into small bowl, pour 1⅓ cups batter; stir in almond extract and food color. Carefully pour pink batter over white batter in pan. Stir chocolate syrup into remaining batter. Carefully pour chocolate batter over pink batter.

4 Bake 40 to 45 minutes or until toothpick inserted 1½ inches from side of cake comes out clean. Cool 10 minutes. Turn pan upside down onto cooling rack or heatproof serving plate; remove pan. Cool completely, about 1 hour.

5 In microwavable bowl, microwave frosting uncovered on High about 15 seconds or until frosting can be stirred smooth and is thin enough to drizzle. Spread over top of cake, allowing some to drizzle down side. Store loosely covered.

1 Serving: Calories 250; Total Fat 8g (Saturated Fat 2g, Trans Fat 0.5g); Cholesterol 0mg; Sodium 320mg; Total Carbohydrate 42g (Dietary Fiber 0g); Protein 2g **Exchanges:** 1 Starch, 2 Other Carbohydrate, 1½ Fat **Carbohydrate Choices:** 3

Sweet Secret Fluted tube cake pans can be a challenge to grease. To make it easier, place a dab of shortening on the outside of a small plastic sandwich bag. Slip the bag onto your hand, and rub shortening on the inside of the pan. Repeat with more shortening until every surface is greased.

Sweet Secret Serve with Neapolitan ice cream, of course!

Upside-Down Mug Cheesecake

1 serving | **PREP TIME: 10 Minutes** | **START TO FINISH: 2 Hours 20 Minutes**

1 egg

2 oz cream cheese, softened

1½ teaspoons heavy whipping cream

2 tablespoons sugar

¾ teaspoon all-purpose flour

¼ teaspoon grated lemon peel

1 tablespoon crushed graham crackers

Additional toppings, if desired (fresh berries, whipped cream, caramel sauce)

1 Spray bottom only of microwavable mug (about 12 oz) with cooking spray. In small bowl, beat egg; remove all but 2 tablespoons (save or discard the removed egg). In the same bowl as the egg, beat cream cheese and whipping cream with whisk until smooth. Add sugar, flour and lemon peel and mix well.

2 Pour batter into mug. Microwave uncovered on Medium (50%) 1 minute 30 seconds, checking and adding an additional 10 to 20 seconds as necessary, until edge slightly pulls away from mug and top is nearly set (cheesecake center may look glossy). Cool 10 minutes. Refrigerate until room temperature, 2 hours.

3 To serve, carefully run knife around edge of cheesecake to loosen; turn onto small plate. Top with crushed graham crackers. Serve with additional toppings, as desired.

1 Serving: Calories 370; Total Fat 23g (Saturated Fat 13g, Trans Fat 0.5g); Cholesterol 75mg; Sodium 300mg; Total Carbohydrate 34g (Dietary Fiber 0g); Protein 7g **Exchanges:** 2½ Other Carbohydrate, 1 Very Lean Meat, 4½ Fat **Carbohydrate Choices:** 2

Sweet Secret This cake is best served chilled. To speed up the chill time, place in freezer 10 to 15 minutes.

Sweet Secret Be sure to cook at 50% power. Microwave ovens vary in cook times, so please start with the minimum cook time, and add time as necessary.

Sweet Secret Spraying only the bottom of the mug with cooking spray will make sure that your cheesecake reaches the proper height during microwaving.

Confetti Mug Cake

1 mug cake | **PREP TIME: 5 Minutes** | **START TO FINISH: 15 Minutes**

CAKE

2	tablespoons butter
½	cup Easy Scratch Cake Mix (page 7)
¼	cup milk
¼	teaspoon vanilla
½	teaspoon confetti decors

FROSTING

¼	cup miniature marshmallows
¼	teaspoon confetti sprinkles

1 In microwavable mug (about 10 oz), microwave butter on High 30 to 45 seconds or until melted. Stir in cake mix, milk and vanilla with fork. Carefully stir in ½ teaspoon confetti until well blended.

2 Microwave on High 1 to 2 minutes or until toothpick inserted in center comes out clean and cake pulls away from side of mug. (Do not overcook.) Cool 5 minutes.

3 Top cake with marshmallows. Microwave on High 20 to 30 seconds or until marshmallows are puffed. Immediately sprinkle with ¼ teaspoon confetti.

1 Mug Cake: Calories 600; Total Fat 25g (Saturated Fat 16g, Trans Fat 1g); Cholesterol 65mg; Sodium 520mg; Total Carbohydrate 85g (Dietary Fiber 1g); Protein 7g **Exchanges:** 2 Starch, 3½ Other Carbohydrate, 5 Fat **Carbohydrate Choices:** 5½

Sweet Secret Make sure that the mug holds at least 10 ounces of liquid or cake may overflow.

Sweet Secret Any of your favorite candy sprinkles can be substituted for the confetti decors in this cake.

Red, White and Blue Poke Cake

16 servings | **PREP TIME: 20 Minutes** | **START TO FINISH: 5 Hours**

1 box white cake mix with pudding

1¼ cups water

⅓ cup vegetable oil

3 egg whites

1 box (4-serving size) strawberry-flavored gelatin

1 cup boiling water

½ cup cold water

1 box (4-serving size) white chocolate instant pudding and pie filling mix

⅓ cup milk

Sweetened Whipped Cream (page 6)

1 cup sliced fresh strawberries

½ cup fresh blueberries

1 Heat oven to 350°F. Make and bake cake mix as directed on box for 13 × 9-inch pan, using water, oil and egg whites. Cool completely in pan on cooling rack, about 1 hour.

2 With long-tined fork, pierce cake every ½ inch. In medium bowl, stir gelatin and boiling water until dissolved. Stir in cold water. Carefully pour mixture over entire surface of cake. Refrigerate at least 3 hours.

3 In large bowl, beat pudding mix and milk with whisk until well blended. Gently stir in whipped cream. Spread over cake. Arrange strawberries and blueberries on top of cake to look like flag. Store loosely covered in refrigerator.

1 Serving: Calories 240; Total Fat 9g (Saturated Fat 3g, Trans Fat 0g); Cholesterol 10mg; Sodium 330mg; Total Carbohydrate 36g (Dietary Fiber 1g); Protein 3g **Exchanges:** 1 Starch, 1½ Other Carbohydrate, 1½ Fat **Carbohydrate Choices:** 2½

Sweet Secret Cut the cake into serving-size pieces and arrange on a platter. Insert a tiny American flag, available at craft stores, into each piece. Garnish the platter with whole strawberries and blueberries.

Sweet Secret You can substitute vanilla pudding mix for the white chocolate pudding mix.

Sweet Secret Substitute 1 container (8 ounces) frozen whipped topping, thawed, for the Sweetened Whipped Cream if you like.

Creating Scrumptious Poke Cakes

Poke cakes are easy to prepare and totable—making them easy to bring to gatherings. The pockets created when poking the cake get filled with eye-catching and delicious fillings that infuse flavor into the cake—how can you miss? It's fun to dive into a forkful of cake, finding the filling surprise. Pump up the flavor and textures of customized poke cakes with the fillings and toppings.

MAKE YOUR POKE MIXTURES PLAY HARD

Adding the right poke mixture to a cake can:

Infuse Flavor to excite your taste buds

Create Contrast with texture and color

Layer Lusciousness between the cake and the topping in one step

POKING PERFECTION

Depending on the texture of the cake and the filling, recipes have different instructions for when to poke and fill the holes in the cake. This is so each cake will have optimum textures for a yummy eating experience.

Poking Cake Too Soon: The cake texture condenses, making it gummy and less fluffy.

Filling Cake Too Soon: The cake becomes gummy or the filling melts.

If you're not sure when to poke and fill, a good guideline is to cool the cake completely before poking and filling it.

THE SCIENCE OF THE POKE

Here's how to choose which method for poking your cake. Poke holes about halfway down into the cake unless noted otherwise in a specific recipe.

Long-Tined Fork: Use for thinner mixtures, and poke the cake no more than every ½ inch so the mixture doesn't make the cake too wet.

Wooden Spoon Handle: Use for thicker mixtures so you can get in more filling (and flavor) per bite. Poke holes about every 1 inch to keep the structure of the cake intact when filled and served.

LAYER UP

When creating a poke cake, think about adding layers of flavor and texture to create interest.

Double Duty: Use a thicker poke mixture and make enough of it to fill not only the holes but also to spread on top of the cake. Pudding or whipped cream–based mixtures work well.

Spread a Topping: Top the poke mixture with a thick layer of Sweetened Whipped Cream (page 6) or frosting. You'll want about 3 cups of Sweetened Whipped Cream or 1 container of frosting to make the layer thick enough.

Sprinkle on the Crunch: Add chopped nuts or seeds, dried bite-size pieces of fruit, crumbled cookies, chopped candy bars, mini chips, toffee bits or sprinkles to the poke mixture, or sprinkle them on top of the finished cake.

Vampire Poke Cake

15 servings | **PREP TIME: 15 Minutes** | **START TO FINISH: 2 Hours**

1 box white cake mix with pudding

1¼ cups water

⅓ cup vegetable oil

3 egg whites

1 cup boiling water

1 box (4-serving size) strawberry-flavored gelatin

1 container fluffy white whipped ready-to-spread frosting

2 tubes (0.68 oz each) red decorating gel

1 Heat oven to 350°F. Spray bottom only of 13 × 9-inch pan with cooking spray.

2 Make and bake cake mix as directed on box for 13 × 9-inch pan, using 1¼ cups water, oil and egg whites. Cool in pan on cooling rack 20 minutes.

3 Meanwhile, in small bowl, pour boiling water over gelatin; stir until gelatin is dissolved. With wooden skewer, poke holes halfway down into warm cake every inch, twisting skewer back and forth. Carefully pour mixture over cake, allowing it to fill in holes. Cool completely on cooling rack, about 1 hour.

4 Spread frosting over cake. Drizzle red decorating gel over frosting. Store covered in refrigerator.

1 Serving: Calories 180; Total Fat 11g (Saturated Fat 3g, Trans Fat 0g); Cholesterol 0mg; Sodium 300mg; Total Carbohydrate 50g (Dietary Fiber 0g); Protein 1g **Exchanges:** 1 Starch, 2 Other Carbohydrate, 2 Fat **Carbohydrate Choices:** 3

Sweet Secret Use your favorite red gelatin in this recipe—cherry, raspberry or watermelon would work well.

Orange Dreamsicle Ice-Cream Cake

10 servings | **PREP TIME: 20 Minutes** | **START TO FINISH: 1 Hour 50 Minutes**

8 cream-filled white snack cakes (from 12.5-oz package)

3 cups orange sherbet, softened

2 cups vanilla ice cream, softened

6 sugar cones (from 5-oz package), coarsely crushed

1 Cut each snack cake horizontally in half; arrange halves in bottom of 9-inch square pan in 4 rows by 4 rows. Spread half of the orange sherbet evenly over cakes. Cover and freeze 30 minutes or until sherbet is firm.

2 Spread vanilla ice cream evenly over orange sherbet. Sprinkle with half of the crushed cones. Cover and freeze 30 minutes or until ice cream is firm.

3 Spread remaining orange sherbet over crushed cones. Sprinkle with remaining crushed cones. Cover and freeze 30 minutes but no longer than 1 week or until sherbet is firm. Cut cake into 2 rows by 5 rows. Store any remaining cake tightly covered in freezer.

1 Serving: Calories 270; Total Fat 8g (Saturated Fat 3g, Trans Fat 0g); Cholesterol 20mg; Sodium 220mg; Total Carbohydrate 47g (Dietary Fiber 1g); Protein 3g **Exchanges:** 1 Starch, 2 Other Carbohydrate, 1½ Fat **Carbohydrate Choices:** 3

Sweet Secret If you like, use a prepared pound cake from the bakery (about 10.75 ounces) instead of the white fancy cakes. Cut pound cake into 1-inch pieces and arrange in single layer in pan.

Simple Sparkle Try other flavor combinations, such as raspberry sherbet with chocolate chip ice cream or lime sherbet with coconut ice cream.

Candy Corn Cupcake Trifles

12 servings | PREP TIME: 25 Minutes | START TO FINISH: 1 Hour 15 Minutes

1   box yellow cake mix with pudding

1   cup water

½   cup vegetable oil

3   eggs

½   teaspoon orange paste food color

¼   teaspoon yellow paste food color

12   mason jars (8-oz size) or other half-pint jars

2   containers fluffy white whipped ready-to-spread frosting

1½   cups candy corn

1 Heat oven to 350°F. Place paper baking cup in each of 24 regular-size muffin cups.

2 Make cake mix as directed on box, using water, oil and eggs. Divide batter in half; tint half of batter orange and other half yellow. Divide each color batter evenly among muffin cups.

3 Bake 18 to 20 minutes or until toothpick inserted in center comes out clean. Cool 10 minutes; remove cupcakes from pans to cooling racks. Cool completely.

4 Remove paper baking cups. Cut each cupcake in half horizontally. In each jar, place 1 yellow cupcake half and 1 orange cupcake half. Spoon 1 container of frosting into 1-gallon resealable food-storage plastic bag; seal bag. Cut off about ½-inch corner of bag. Twist bag above frosting; squeeze bag to pipe frosting over orange cupcake in each jar. Sprinkle evenly with 1 cup of the candy corn. Repeat layers with remaining cupcake halves, second container of frosting and remaining ½ cup candy corn.

1 Serving: Calories 603; Total Fat 24g (Saturated Fat 5g, Trans Fat 0g); Cholesterol 0mg; Sodium 413mg; Total Carbohydrate 92g (Dietary Fiber 0g); Protein 2g **Exchanges:** 1 Starch, 4½ Other Carbohydrate, 4½ Fat **Carbohydrate Choices:** 5½

Sweet Secret You can use regular candy corn or "harvest" candy corn, which has brown, orange and white colors.

Angel Food Cake Shakes

2 servings | **PREP TIME: 10 Minutes** | **START TO FINISH: 10 Minutes**

2 cups vanilla frozen yogurt, slightly softened

¼ cup milk

1 1½-inch slice prepared angel food cake, torn into pieces (about 1½ cups)

Sweetened Whipped Cream (page 6), if desired

Fresh berries, if desired

1 In blender, place yogurt and milk. Cover and blend on high speed until smooth and creamy. Add cake pieces; cover and blend until smooth, stopping blender to scrape down sides if necessary.

2 Pour into 2 glasses. Top with whipped cream and berries. Serve immediately.

1 Serving: Calories 380; Total Fat 5g (Saturated Fat 3g, Trans Fat 0g); Cholesterol 20mg; Sodium 430mg; Total Carbohydrate 69g (Dietary Fiber 0g); Protein 14g **Exchanges:** 1 Starch, 2½ Other Carbohydrate, 1½ Skim Milk, ½ Fat **Carbohydrate Choices:** 4½

Sweet Secret Trim the fat and calories in this shake by using fat-free frozen yogurt and skim milk.

Sweet Secret Use this recipe when you have leftover angel food cake on hand.

Simple Sparkle Drizzle with chocolate or strawberry syrup for a pretty presentation.

Angel Food Flag Cake

16 servings | **PREP TIME: 45 Minutes** | **START TO FINISH: 4 Hours 30 Minutes**

1 package white angel food cake mix

1¼ cups cold water

3 cups fresh or frozen unsweetened (thawed and drained) raspberries

3 tablespoons sugar

3 tablespoons seedless red raspberry jam, melted

Sweetened Whipped Cream (page 6)

2 cups fresh or frozen (thawed and drained) blueberries

1 Move oven rack to middle position. Heat oven to 350°F.

2 In extra-large bowl, beat cake mix and 1¼ cups cold water with electric mixer on low speed 30 seconds, then on medium speed 1 minute. Pour into 2 ungreased 9 × 5-inch loaf pans or 3 ungreased 8 × 4-inch loaf pans.

3 Bake 9 × 5-inch loaf pans 35 to 45 minutes, 8 × 4-inch loaf pans 28 to 38 minutes, or until tops are dark golden brown and cracks feel very dry and not sticky. Immediately turn each pan on its side on heatproof surface; let rest until completely cool, about 1 hour. Run knife around sides of pans to loosen cakes; remove from pans to a cutting board.

4 Using the same loaf pans, line each with plastic wrap, allowing wrap to extend over edges. Place raspberries, sugar and jam in food processor; cover and process, using three quick on-and-off motions, until coarsely chopped. Using serrated or electric knife, cut each loaf cake horizontally into 4 slices. Place 1 slice in bottom of each pan; spread 3 tablespoons of the raspberry mixture over each. Top with a second cake slice. Repeat with remaining raspberry mixture and cake slices. Cover with plastic wrap and refrigerate at least 2 hours or until chilled but no longer than 24 hours.

5 To remove loaves easily from pans, place serving plate upside down on top of pan; turn pan upside down onto plate. Remove pan and plastic wrap. Using serrated or electric knife, cut each loaf crosswise into 8 slices. Serve with whipped cream and blueberries.

1 Serving: Calories 180; Total Fat 3g (Saturated Fat 1.5g, Trans Fat 0g); Cholesterol 10mg; Sodium 250mg; Total Carbohydrate 35g (Dietary Fiber 2g); Protein 2g **Exchanges:** ½ Starch, 2 Other Carbohydrate, ½ Fat **Carbohydrate Choices:** 2

Sweet Secret Fresh or frozen unsweetened strawberries and seedless strawberry jam are good alternatives to the raspberries and raspberry jam.

Sweet Secret If you prefer, you can substitute 1 container (8 ounces) frozen whipped topping, thawed, for the Sweetened Whipped Cream.

Party Ice-Cream Cake

16 servings | **PREP TIME: 10 Minutes** | **START TO FINISH: 5 Hours 45 Minutes**

1 box party rainbow chip
cake mix with pudding

1¼ cups water

⅓ cup vegetable oil

3 eggs

1 quart frozen yogurt (any
flavor), slightly softened

Candy decorations, fresh
fruit or whipped cream,
as desired

1 Heat oven to 350°F. Make, bake and cool cake as directed on box for 13 × 9-inch pan, using water, oil and eggs.

2 Spread frozen yogurt over top of cake. Immediately cover; freeze at least 4 hours until firm.

3 Just before serving, top each serving as desired. Cover and freeze any remaining cake.

1 Serving: Calories 240; Total Fat 10g (Saturated Fat 2.5g, Trans Fat 0g); Cholesterol 45mg; Sodium 250mg; Total Carbohydrate 34g (Dietary Fiber 0g); Protein 4g **Exchanges:** 2 Other Carbohydrate, ½ Milk, 1 Fat **Carbohydrate Choices:** 2

Sweet Secret Use your favorite flavor of frozen yogurt, ice cream or sherbet to "frost" this festive rainbow chip cake.

Sweet Secret So the frozen cake won't be too hard to cut, remove it from the freezer 20 to 30 minutes before serving.

Unicorn Doughnut Cake

8 servings | **PREP TIME: 25 Minutes** | **START TO FINISH: 8 Hours 25 Minutes**

1½ cups heavy whipping cream

1 package (8 oz) cream cheese, softened

1 cup sugar

1 teaspoon vanilla

Purple, blue and pink gel food colors

6 purchased cake doughnuts, cut horizontally in half

3 tablespoons star decorating decors

2 teaspoons white edible glitter

1 Line 9 x 5-inch loaf pan with plastic wrap, allowing wrap to extend over edges.

2 In large chilled bowl, beat whipping cream with electric mixer on low speed until cream begins to thicken. Gradually increase speed to high and beat just until stiff peaks form; set aside. In another large bowl, beat cream cheese, sugar and vanilla with electric mixer on medium speed 1 to 2 minutes or until smooth and creamy.

3 Fold whipped cream into cream cheese mixture until well blended. Divide cream cheese mixture evenly among 3 bowls, about 1½ cups each. Using food colors, tint batter in 1 bowl purple, 1 bowl blue and 1 bowl pink.

4 Place 3 doughnut halves cut side up in bottom of loaf pan. Cut fourth doughnut half into pieces, to fit in pan. Spread purple cream evenly over doughnuts. Sprinkle with 1 tablespoon of the star decors. Repeat with 4 doughnut halves, the blue cream and 1 tablespoon star decors. Top with remaining 4 doughnut halves, the pink cream and remaining star decors. Sprinkle with edible glitter. Cover and refrigerate at least 8 hours but no longer than 48 hours.

1 Serving: Calories 530; Total Fat 35g (Saturated Fat 19g, Trans Fat 2.5g); Cholesterol 105mg; Sodium 200mg; Total Carbohydrate 48g (Dietary Fiber 0g); Protein 5g **Exchanges:** 1½ Starch, 1½ Other Carbohydrate, 7 Fat **Carbohydrate Choices:** 3

Sweet Secret Use any combination of your favorite pastel gel food colors for the cream in this cake.

Simple Sparkle This cake would be a smash hit at a girl's birthday party or sleepover. Serve it with a scoop of brightly colored sherbet for an eye-catching dessert.

Toffee-S'mores Icebox Cake

8 servings | **PREP TIME: 25 Minutes** | **START TO FINISH: 8 Hours 35 Minutes**

11 graham crackers (from 14.4-oz box)

1 box (4-serving size) instant chocolate pudding and pie filling mix

2 cups milk

1½ cups heavy whipping cream

1 cup marshmallow creme

1 cup milk chocolate toffee bits (from 8-oz package)

½ cup miniature marshmallows (from 10.5-oz package)

½ cup hot fudge sauce

1 Line 9 × 5-inch loaf pan with foil, allowing foil to extend over edges.

2 In small bowl, crumble 2 graham crackers (reserve remaining 9 crackers); set aside. Prepare pudding mix as directed on box, using milk; set aside. In medium bowl, beat whipping cream with electric mixer on low speed until cream begins to thicken. Gradually increase speed to high and beat just until stiff peaks form; fold in marshmallow creme.

3 Line bottom of pan with 3 graham crackers, breaking in half and overlapping to fit. Spread 1 cup of the whipped cream mixture evenly over crackers. Repeat another layer with 3 graham crackers and 1 cup of the pudding spread evenly over crackers. Sprinkle with ½ cup toffee bits. Top with remaining 3 graham crackers, the remaining pudding and whipped cream mixture. Sprinkle with crumbled graham crackers and remaining ½ cup toffee bits.

4 Sprinkle marshmallows evenly over top of cake. Set oven control to broil. Broil with cake top about 6 inches from heat about 1 minute or until marshmallows are golden brown (watch carefully so marshmallows don't burn). Freeze at least 8 hours until firm but no longer than 1 week.

5 To serve, use foil to lift cake from pan to serving platter; remove foil. Let stand 10 minutes before serving. Drizzle each serving with 1 tablespoon hot fudge sauce.

1 Serving: Calories 620; Total Fat 32g (Saturated Fat 17g, Trans Fat 1g); Cholesterol 65mg; Sodium 420mg; Total Carbohydrate 76g (Dietary Fiber 1g); Protein 6g **Exchanges:** 2 Starch, 3 Other Carbohydrate, 6 Fat **Carbohydrate Choices:** 5

Simple Sparkle Add another layer of flavor and texture by sprinkling servings of the cake with toasted coconut before serving—yum!

Peanutty Ice-Cream Cookie Cake

16 servings | PREP TIME: 15 Minutes | START TO FINISH: 5 Hours 40 Minutes

1 pouch (1 lb 1.5 oz) double chocolate chunk cookie mix

⅓ cup hot fudge topping

¼ cup vegetable oil

1 egg

4 cups vanilla ice cream or frozen yogurt, softened

¼ cup caramel topping

1 cup peanuts

1 Heat oven to 350°F. Lightly spray 10-inch springform pan with cooking spray. Or line 9-inch square pan with foil, leaving about 2 inches of foil overhanging two opposite sides of pan; lightly spray with cooking spray.

2 In large bowl, stir cookie mix, 2 tablespoons of the hot fudge topping, the oil and egg until soft dough forms. Press dough in bottom and 1 inch up sides of pan.

3 Bake 13 to 15 minutes or until top of crust is no longer shiny. Cool completely, about 1 hour.

4 Spread ice cream over cookie crust. Freeze 2 hours. Drizzle with caramel topping and remaining hot fudge topping; sprinkle with peanuts. Freeze at least 2 hours longer or until firm, up to 1 week.

5 To serve, remove sides of springform pan, or use foil to lift dessert out of 9-inch pan. Let stand 10 minutes. Use hot wet knife to cut into wedges or squares. Store covered in freezer.

1 Serving: Calories 330; Total Fat 15g (Saturated Fat 5g, Trans Fat 0g); Cholesterol 30mg; Sodium 280mg; Total Carbohydrate 42g (Dietary Fiber 1g); Protein 5g **Exchanges:** 1 Starch, 2 Other Carbohydrate, 3 Fat **Carbohydrate Choices:** 3

Sweet Secret If caramel and hot fudge toppings are too thick to drizzle, place in separate small microwavable bowls. Microwave each on High 20 to 30 seconds until of drizzling consistency.

Sweet Secret Use your favorite ice-cream flavor in this frozen cake.

No-Bake Samoa Cake

16 servings | **PREP TIME: 30 Minutes** | **START TO FINISH: 4 Hours 30 Minutes**

1   cup packed brown sugar

½   cup butter

1   can (14 oz) sweetened condensed milk (not evaporated)

2   boxes (4-serving size) instant coconut pudding and pie filling mix

2¾   cups milk

1½   cups whipping cream

2   packages (11.2 oz each) shortbread cookies, coarsely crushed (about 6 cups)

1   cup coconut, toasted

½   cup chopped pecans, toasted

1   cup hot fudge sauce

1 In 2-quart saucepan, cook brown sugar, butter and sweetened condensed milk over medium heat until butter is melted, stirring constantly. Reduce heat to low; cook 4 minutes, stirring constantly. Refrigerate 15 minutes.

2 Meanwhile, prepare pudding as directed on box using 2¾ cups milk. Set aside.

3 In chilled medium bowl, beat whipping cream with electric mixer on low speed until cream begins to thicken. Gradually increase speed to high and beat just until soft peaks form. Gently fold whipped cream and ½ cup of the coconut into pudding.

4 Place 3 cups of the cookie crumbs in bottom of an ungreased 13 × 9-inch (3-quart) glass baking dish. Spoon half of the pudding mixture evenly on top of cookies. Sprinkle 1 cup of the cookie crumbs over pudding mixture. Pour sweetened condensed milk mixture evenly onto cookie crumbs. Top with remaining 2 cups cookie crumbs and the pudding mixture. Sprinkle with remaining ½ cup coconut and the pecans. Cover and refrigerate 3 to 4 hours or until chilled but no longer than 48 hours. Serve with hot fudge sauce.

1 Serving: Calories 650; Total Fat 31g (Saturated Fat 15g, Trans Fat 3g); Cholesterol 60mg; Sodium 600mg; Total Carbohydrate 83g (Dietary Fiber 2g); Protein 7g **Exchanges:** 1 Starch, 4 Other Carbohydrate, ½ Milk, 5½ Fat **Carbohydrate Choices:** 5½

Sweet Secret Substitute 3 cups frozen whipped topping (thawed) for the whipping cream in this recipe if you like.

Sweet Secret To crush cookies, place in 1-gallon resealable food-storage plastic bag; seal bag. Using meat mallet or rolling pin, crush cookies. Break up larger pieces if necessary.

Sweet Secret To toast coconut and pecans, sprinkle in separate ungreased heavy skillets. Cook over medium heat 5 to 7 minutes, stirring frequently until they begin to brown, then stirring constantly until they are light brown.

Mojito Cake

15 servings | **PREP TIME: 30 Minutes** | **START TO FINISH: 2 Hours 20 Minutes**

CAKE

- 1 box white cake mix with pudding
- 1 cup unflavored carbonated water
- ⅓ cup vegetable oil
- ¼ cup rum or 1 teaspoon rum extract plus ¼ cup water
- 3 tablespoons chopped fresh mint leaves
- 2 teaspoons grated lime peel
- 3 egg whites

GLAZE

- ½ cup butter
- ¼ cup water
- 1 cup granulated sugar
- ½ cup rum or 2 teaspoons rum extract plus ½ cup water

GARNISH

- 1 cup whipping cream
- 2 tablespoons powdered sugar
- 15 fresh mint leaves, if desired
- Shredded lime peel, if desired

1 Heat oven to 350°F. Grease bottom only of 13 × 9-inch pan with shortening; lightly flour.

2 In large bowl, beat cake ingredients with electric mixer on low speed 30 seconds, then on medium speed 2 minutes, scraping bowl occasionally. Pour batter into pan.

3 Bake as directed on box for 13 × 9-inch pan. Cool 15 minutes.

4 Meanwhile, in 2-quart saucepan, mix glaze ingredients. Heat to boiling over high heat, stirring frequently. Reduce heat to medium; continue to boil 3 minutes, stirring frequently, until glaze has thickened slightly.

5 With long-tined fork or toothpick, poke holes halfway down into cake every ½-inch. Gradually pour glaze over cake. Cool completely, about 1 hour.

6 In small bowl, beat whipping cream and powdered sugar with electric mixer on high speed until soft peaks form. Garnish each serving with whipped cream, mint leaf and shredded lime peel. Store cake loosely covered.

1 Serving: Calories 350; Total Fat 17g (Saturated Fat 8g, Trans Fat 0g); Cholesterol 35mg; Sodium 270mg; Total Carbohydrate 41g (Dietary Fiber 0g); Protein 2g **Exchanges:** ½ Starch, 2½ Other Carbohydrate, 3½ Fat **Carbohydrate Choices:** 3

Sweet Secret In a pinch, use purchased frozen whipped topping, thawed, instead of making your own whipped cream.

Spooky Ghost Cupcakes

24 cupcakes | **PREP TIME: 1 Hour** | **START TO FINISH: 1 Hour 50 Minutes**

1 box chocolate fudge cake mix with pudding

1¼ cups water

½ cup vegetable oil

3 eggs

2 containers vanilla creamy ready-to-spread frosting

½ cup candy sprinkles or colored sugar

1 package (0.88 oz) candy eyeballs

1 Heat oven to 375°F. Place paper baking cup in each of 24 regular-size muffin cups. Make and bake cake mix using water, oil and eggs as directed on box for 24 cupcakes. Cool completely, about 30 minutes.

2 Frost cupcakes a few at a time using 1 container frosting. Immediately sprinkle cupcakes with decors.

3 Place contents of second container of frosting in quart-size resealable freezer plastic bag. Cut small tip from corner of bag. Squeeze frosting onto cupcakes in mound shapes of various sizes.

4 Decorate as desired using candy eyeballs on frosting mounds.

1 Cupcake: Calories 280; Total Fat 12g (Saturated Fat 4g, Trans Fat 0g); Cholesterol 25mg; Sodium 250mg; Total Carbohydrate 44g (Dietary Fiber 0g); Protein 1g **Exchanges:** 3 Other Carbohydrate, 2½ Fat **Carbohydrate Choices:** 3

Sweet Secret If you don't have candy eyeballs, you can use mini chocolate chips instead.

Sweet Secret You can use disposable plastic decorating bags for adding the mounds of frosting.

Simple Sparkle Add a few drops of neon food color to the frosting for a festive look. Get creative, and decorate cupcakes as you like.

Strawberry Jam Tiny Toast Cakes

60 mini cupcakes | **PREP TIME: 1 Hour** | **START TO FINISH: 1 Hour 35 Minutes**

1 box yellow cake mix with pudding

1 cup water

½ cup vegetable oil

3 eggs

½ cup strawberry jam

1 container vanilla whipped ready-to-spread frosting

1¼ cups Strawberry Toast Crunch™ cereal

Red nonpareils or candy sprinkles

1 Heat oven to 350°F. Place mini paper baking cup in each of 60 mini muffin cups.

2 Make cake batter as directed on box using water, oil and eggs. Fill muffin cups three-fourths full (about 1 heaping tablespoon each).

3 Bake 10 to 15 minutes or until toothpick inserted in center of cupcake comes out clean. Cool 5 minutes; remove from pans to cooling racks. Cool completely, about 15 minutes.

4 With handle of wooden spoon, slowly twist back and forth into top of each cupcake to make ½-inch-wide indentation not quite to bottom, wiping spoon handle occasionally if necessary.

5 Spoon jam into small resealable food-storage plastic bag; seal bag. Cut ¼-inch tip off 1 bottom corner of bag. Insert tip of bag into opening in each cupcake; squeeze bag to fill indentation.

6 Frost cupcakes. Garnish each with cereal pieces and sprinkles.

1 Mini Cupcake: Calories 90; Total Fat 4g (Saturated Fat 1.5g, Trans Fat 0g); Cholesterol 10mg; Sodium 65mg; Total Carbohydrate 12g (Dietary Fiber 0g); Protein 0g **Exchanges:** 1 Other Carbohydrate, 1 Fat **Carbohydrate Choices:** 1

Sweet Secret For a peanut butter and jam twist, spoon ¼ cup creamy peanut butter into small resealable food-storage plastic bag; seal bag. Cut ¼-inch tip off 1 bottom corner of bag. Insert tip of bag into opening in each cupcake; squeeze bag to fill indentation halfway with peanut butter. Fill remaining half with ¼ cup strawberry jam.

Sweet Secret Try blueberry Tiny Toast cereal with blueberry preserves for a fun flavor twist.

Snickerdoodle Cupcakes

24 cupcakes | **PREP TIME: 40 Minutes** | **START TO FINISH: 1 Hour 35 Minutes**

CUPCAKES

2¾	cups all-purpose flour
3	teaspoons baking powder
1	teaspoon ground cinnamon
½	teaspoon salt
¾	cup shortening
1⅔	cups granulated sugar
5	egg whites
2½	teaspoons vanilla
1¼	cups milk

FROSTING

6	cups powdered sugar
2	teaspoons ground cinnamon
⅔	cup butter, softened
1	tablespoon vanilla
2 to 4	tablespoons milk

GARNISH

2	teaspoons granulated sugar
½	teaspoon ground cinnamon

1 Heat oven to 350°F. Place paper baking cup in each of 24 regular-size muffin cups.

2 In medium bowl, mix flour, baking powder, 1 teaspoon cinnamon and the salt; set aside.

3 In large bowl, beat shortening with electric mixer on medium speed 30 seconds. Gradually add 1⅔ cups granulated sugar, about ⅓ cup at a time, beating well after each addition and scraping bowl occasionally. Beat 2 minutes longer. Add egg whites, one at a time, beating well after each addition. Beat in 2½ teaspoons vanilla. On low speed, alternately add flour mixture, about one-third at a time, and 1¼ cups milk, about half at a time, beating just until blended.

4 Divide batter evenly among muffin cups, filling each with about 3 tablespoons batter (about two-thirds full).

5 Bake 18 to 20 minutes or until toothpick inserted in center comes out clean. Cool 5 minutes. Remove from pans to cooling racks. Cool completely, about 30 minutes.

6 In large bowl, mix powdered sugar, 2 teaspoons cinnamon and the butter with electric mixer on low speed until smooth. Beat in 1 tablespoon vanilla and 2 tablespoons milk. Gradually beat in enough remaining milk, 1 teaspoon at a time, to make frosting smooth and spreadable. Frost cooled cupcakes. In small bowl, mix garnish ingredients; sprinkle over frosted cupcakes.

1 Cupcake: Calories 350; Total Fat 12g (Saturated Fat 5g, Trans Fat 1.5g); Cholesterol 15mg; Sodium 160mg; Total Carbohydrate 56g (Dietary Fiber 0g); Protein 2g **Exchanges:** ½ Starch, 3 Other Carbohydrate, 2½ Fat **Carbohydrate Choices:** 4

Two-Ingredient Soda Pop Cupcakes

24 cupcakes | **PREP TIME: 10 Minutes** | **START TO FINISH: 1 Hour 45 Minutes**

1 box white cake mix
  with pudding
1 can (12 oz) carbonated
  beverage of choice

1 Heat oven to 350°F. Place paper baking cup in each of 24 regular-size muffin cups.

2 In large bowl, beat cake mix and carbonated beverage with electric mixer on low speed 1 minute, then on medium speed 2 minutes, scraping side of bowl. Divide batter evenly among cups.

3 Bake 15 to 18 minutes or until toothpick inserted in center comes out clean. Cool 10 minutes; remove from pans to cooling racks. Cool completely, about 1 hour.

1 Cupcake: Calories 80; Total Fat 1g (Saturated Fat 0g, Trans Fat 0g); Cholesterol 0mg; Sodium 135mg; Total Carbohydrate 17g (Dietary Fiber 0g); Protein 1g **Exchanges:** 1 Other Carbohydrate **Carbohydrate Choices:** 1

Sweet Secret For best results, use a fruit-flavored carbonated beverage, such as orange, grape, strawberry or lemon-lime.

Simple Sparkle Frost with your favorite ready-to-spread frosting, tinted orange with a few drops of food color and a dollop of whipped cream, if you like. Garnish with paper straws for a bit of fun.

Halloween Candy Cupcakes

24 cupcakes | PREP TIME: 20 Minutes | START TO FINISH: 1 Hour 55 Minutes

1 box devil's food cake mix with pudding

1¼ cups water

½ cup vegetable oil

3 eggs

1 cup miniature semisweet chocolate chips

1 container vanilla creamy ready-to-spread frosting

1 cup candy-coated chocolate candies

20 miniature chocolate-covered peanut butter cup candies, unwrapped, chopped

1 cup candy corn

1 Heat oven to 350°F. Place paper baking cup in each of 24 regular-size muffin cups.

2 Make cake mix as directed on box, using water, oil and eggs. Fold in chocolate chips. Divide batter evenly among muffin cups.

3 Bake 18 to 24 minutes or until toothpick inserted in center comes out clean. Cool 10 minutes; remove from pans to cooling racks. Cool completely, about 1 hour.

4 Frost cupcakes. Sprinkle candy-coated chocolate candies, peanut butter cup candies and candy corn evenly over cupcakes.

1 Serving: Calories 340; Total Fat 15g (Saturated Fat 5g, Trans Fat 0g); Cholesterol 0mg; Sodium 250mg; Total Carbohydrate 51g (Dietary Fiber 1g); Protein 3g **Exchanges:** ½ Starch, 3 Other Carbohydrate, 3 Fat **Carbohydrate Choices:** 3½

Simple Sparkle Use your favorite Halloween treats to top these chock-full-of-candy cupcakes.

Ginger-Spice Cupcakes with Cream Cheese Frosting

18 cupcakes | **PREP TIME: 40 Minutes** | **START TO FINISH: 1 Hour 25 Minutes**

CUPCAKES

- ½ cup granulated sugar
- ½ cup butter, softened
- ½ cup molasses
- 2 eggs
- 2 cups white whole wheat flour
- 1 teaspoon baking soda
- ½ teaspoon salt
- 1½ teaspoons ground ginger
- ½ teaspoon ground cinnamon
- ½ teaspoon ground allspice
- ¾ cup water

FROSTING

- 1 package (8 oz) cream cheese, softened
- ¼ cup butter, softened
- 2 teaspoons grated lemon peel
- 1 teaspoon ground cinnamon
- 1 teaspoon vanilla
- 4 cups (1 lb) powdered sugar
- 1 to 2 teaspoons milk

1 Heat oven to 375°F. Place paper baking cup in each of 18 regular-size muffin cups.

2 In large bowl, beat granulated sugar, ½ cup butter, the molasses and eggs with electric mixer on medium speed, or mix with spoon, until well blended. Stir in flour, baking soda, salt, ginger, ½ teaspoon cinnamon, the allspice and water. Spoon about ¼ cup batter into each muffin cup.

3 Bake 15 to 18 minutes or until toothpick inserted in center comes out clean. Cool 5 minutes. Remove from pans to cooling racks. Cool completely, about 20 minutes.

4 Meanwhile, in medium bowl, beat cream cheese, ¼ cup butter, the lemon peel, 1 teaspoon cinnamon and the vanilla with electric mixer on low speed until smooth. Gradually beat in powdered sugar, 1 cup at a time, until smooth. Beat in milk, 1 teaspoon at a time, until spreadable.

5 Pipe or spread generous amount of frosting on top of each cupcake. Sprinkle lightly with cinnamon if desired. Store covered in refrigerator.

1 Cupcake: Calories 312.2; Total Fat 13g (Saturated Fat 7.5g, Trans Fat 0g); Cholesterol 55mg; Sodium 194mg; Total Carbohydrate 48g (Dietary Fiber 2g); Protein 3g **Exchanges:** 1 Starch; 2½ Other; 2½ Fat **Carbohydrate Choices:** 3

Sweet Secret This recipe uses white whole wheat flour, which has a light taste and color, but you can substitute regular whole wheat flour if you prefer.

Simple Sparkle Sprinkle the frosting with ground cinnamon.

Metric Conversion Guide

VOLUME

U.S. UNITS	CANADIAN METRIC	AUSTRALIAN METRIC
¼ teaspoon	1 mL	1 ml
½ teaspoon	2 mL	2 ml
1 teaspoon	5 mL	5 ml
1 tablespoon	15 mL	20 ml
¼ cup	50 mL	60 ml
⅓ cup	75 mL	80 ml
½ cup	125 mL	125 ml
⅔ cup	150 mL	170 ml
¾ cup	175 mL	190 ml
1 cup	250 mL	250 ml
1 quart	1 liter	1 liter
1½ quarts	1.5 liters	1.5 liters
2 quarts	2 liters	2 liters
2½ quarts	2.5 liters	2.5 liters
3 quarts	3 liters	3 liters
4 quarts	4 liters	4 liters

WEIGHT

U.S. UNITS	CANADIAN METRIC	AUSTRALIAN METRIC
1 ounce	30 grams	30 grams
2 ounces	55 grams	60 grams
3 ounces	85 grams	90 grams
4 ounces (¼ pound)	115 grams	125 grams
8 ounces (½ pound)	225 grams	225 grams
16 ounces (1 pound)	455 grams	500 grams
1 pound	455 grams	0.5 kilogram

Note: The recipes in this cookbook have not been developed or tested using metric measures. When converting recipes to metric, some variations in quality may be noted.

MEASUREMENTS

INCHES	CENTIMETERS
1	2.5
2	5.0
3	7.5
4	10.0
5	12.5
6	15.0
7	17.5
8	20.5
9	23.0
10	25.5
11	28.0
12	30.5
13	33.0

TEMPERATURES

FAHRENHEIT	CELSIUS
32°	0°
212°	100°
250°	120°
275°	140°
300°	150°
325°	160°
350°	180°
375°	190°
400°	200°
425°	220°
450°	230°
475°	240°
500°	260°

INDEX

Note: Page references in *italics* indicate photographs.

Recipe Testing and Calculating Nutrition Information

RECIPE TESTING:

- Large eggs and 2% milk were used unless otherwise indicated.

- Fat-free, low-fat, low-sodium or lite products were not used unless indicated.

- No nonstick cookware and bakeware were used unless otherwise indicated. No dark-colored, black or insulated bakeware was used.

- When a pan is specified, a metal pan was used; a baking dish or pie plate means ovenproof glass was used.

- An electric hand mixer was used for mixing only when mixer speeds are specified.

CALCULATING NUTRITION:

- The first ingredient was used wherever a choice is given, such as ⅓ cup sour cream or plain yogurt.

- The first amount was used wherever a range is given, such as 3- to 3½-pound whole chicken.

- The first serving number was used wherever a range is given, such as 4 to 6 servings.

- "If desired" ingredients were not included.

- Only the amount of a marinade or frying oil that is absorbed was included.

- Diabetic exchanges are not calculated in recipes containing uncooked alcohol due to its effect on blood sugar levels.